English Composition

English Composition

Connect, Collaborate, Communicate

ANN INOSHITA, KARYL GARLAND, KATE SIMS, JEANNE K. TSUTSUI KEUMA, AND TASHA WILLIAMS

HONOLULU

Print ISBN 978-1-948027-06-9

Ebook ISBN 978-1-948027-07-6

This book was produced with Pressbooks (https://pressbooks.com) and rendered with Prince.

Contents

Foreword

Open Educational Resources (OER) are course materials that are free of cost and come with an intellectual property license that permits reuse and repurposing. It is important to make OER available at colleges and universities because students benefit by having access to essential course content without the cost of purchasing expensive textbooks.

This OER textbook has been designed for students to learn the foundational concepts for first-year college writing. In May 2019, English writing instructors from various campuses in the University of Hawai'i (UH) system—Karyl Garland (University of Hawai'i at Mānoa [UHM]), Ann Inoshita (Leeward Community College), Jeanne K. Tsutsui Keuma (Leeward Community College, Wai'anae Moku), Kate Sims (Hawai'i Community College, Pālamanui), and Tasha S. Williams (Leeward Community College)—collaborated to create this OER textbook. They were given three days and nights to complete a comprehensive, robust text that contains essential concepts for first-year writing at the college level, with facilitation support and copyediting from Book Sprints, the UHM Outreach College OER Project, and the UH ITS Online Learning team.

The team of instructors compared the learning objectives for first-year writing from across UH campuses system-wide. Although each campus had its own respective language regarding student learning objectives, there were many commonalities. Thus, for this textbook, we created the following learning objectives.

After reading this text and applying writing skills, students should be able do the following:

Image by Ann Inoshita

- Demonstrate college-level writing on an assigned topic, with a clear purpose, in a form appropriate for an intended audience.
- Demonstrate critical thinking, effective use of study and college-success skills.
- Use a multi-step, recursive writing process that includes prewriting, drafting, editing, proofreading, and revising, including making use of written and oral feedback.
- Apply to writing the rules and conventions of grammar, word choice, punctuation, and spelling.
- Compose complex and well-reasoned essays that incorporate credible source materials following an appropriate style guide.

The content of this textbook is aimed at helping students meet these learning objectives. This textbook contains five sections: (1) Success Skills for College Learning and Intellectual Growth, (2) The Writing Process, (3) Essay Structure, (4) Types of Essays, and (5) Research Skills.

We wish you well on your academic journey, and we hope this First-Year Writing OER textbook supports you throughout your first college writing course and beyond.

—Karyl Garland, Ann Inoshita, Jeanne K. Tsutsui Keuma, Kate Sims, and Tasha Williams

CHAPTER 1. COLLEGE SUCCESS SKILLS

1.1 Introduction

Image by Kyle Gregory Devaras on Unsplash

Learning Objectives

Students will be able to achieve the following after reading this chapter:

- Understand the habits, behaviors, mindsets, perspectives and overall college success skills students need to practice to achieve academic goals.
- Use skills to communicate effectively, proactively, diplomatically, professionally, and in a timely manner with instructors and peers.
- Understand the top nine intellectual standards for quality thinking, speaking, and writing and apply them to college studies.
- Demonstrate an understanding of the differences between "growth" and "fixed" mindsets and of how to

apply the growth mindset for greater college success.

A Student's Story

Josh started college after being injured while working in construction. He hoped to earn a teaching degree and to work in a career that fit his family life. He thought that, given his past job—rising at an early hour, arriving on time, and working hard throughout an 8- to 10-hour day—he would find it easy to take on a full-time schedule of classes at the local community college. However, as the semester began, he struggled to maintain his weekly one-hour physical therapy appointments on top of 15 hours per week in the classroom, 5 hours per week of commuting to and from college, 25–36 hours per week of reading and studying for quizzes and class discussions, and still taking care of family and personal needs. He lost hours of sleep and found it difficult to stay awake in classes.

He considered dropping a course and decided to see his academic counselor. She took great care to speak with Josh about college success skills, starting with creating and adhering to a manageable schedule that would ensure that he had time for effective studying, for his personal needs, and especially for his family—the people for whom he had committed himself to earning a degree and becoming a teacher.

It's important for students like Josh to know that they are not alone in dealing with these kinds of challenges and frustrations. Not only is he in similar company with other adult students (i.e., who are either returning to college or have decided to change paths and start their college career with the professional world in mind), but also with many college freshmen just out of high school (i.e., who are just beginning the academic transition from high school). Regardless of a student's situation, each needs to develop specific behaviors, habits, and mindsets to succeed in college-level courses and to successfully earn the degree desired.

Students must learn the art of balance. Balancing life with one's college career is challenging, but so is balancing life as an adult. If students value working in their desired careers, the college effort is worth the career rewards, along with the many subsequent benefits accrued over a lifetime. As former First Lady Michelle Obama said when she reminded students of the true and eternal value of taking academic strides:

> There is nothing that any of you can't do. This is what you have to do. You have to stay in school. You have to. You have to go to college. You have to get your degree [b]ecause...the one thing people can't take away from you is your education. And it is worth the investment. So stay focused. (Obama, pars. 33-34)

1.2 College Success Skills

It's About Time: Attendance and "Presence"

In elementary school, children are reminded to "stay on task" and focus on classroom activities. But college students often need to remind themselves of this as well—to maintain focus and develop the set of skills needed to help them find success in college and achieve their dreams.

College students are expected to demonstrate independence, responsibility, and relationship-building skills. While elementary-school students are dropped off and picked up from school by adults, college students are now the adults and are on their own. Adults make decisions about being early or on time to classes and meetings; balancing the shifting priorities of home life, work life, and school life; and reaching their destinations even when their cars won't start.

For college freshmen, whatever their age, the first year in college is a big transition and a learning experience in itself. Many students find themselves unable to catch up after missing even a single class. Class time is learning time.

In every class session, instructors cover course content, and students are invited (and expected) to think about the information, take notes, and participate in class discussions. Instructors, regardless of the level and subject they teach, want their students to learn things of value and that extend beyond the classroom and grade into the professional and the wider world. Most instructors put concerted and contemplative time and effort into what will become their teaching time, so they expect students to be in class to gain all they can.

However, sometimes students are absent when unforeseen events and challenges occur. So from the very first day of a student's college career, the student needs to be courageous and conscientious, to contact instructors and proactively notify them in advance of every absence, to express regret, and to show a commitment to moving forward. This is particularly critical if colleges use an automatic drop or withdrawal system that cancels students' registration if they are absent for two straight weeks.

Whether via email, phone call, text, or even in person, students should notify all their instructors about any potential missed day of class. Regardless of the notification method, students shouldn't ask what they missed. For example, in the email text below, line 3 is a faux pas.

1 *Good afternoon, Professor McKenna.*

2 *I had a family emergency today and was unable to make it to campus.*

3 *Did I miss anything important? If so, is there a time I could meet with you?*

4 *I look forward to your response.*

5 *Josh McDonald*

6 *English 100, Section 006, Tuesday & Thursday, 3:00 p.m.–4:15 p.m.*

7 *Cell: 777-123-4567*

Students can be certain that "something important" was definitely covered that day in class and that it's not the instructor's responsibility to teach it twice; however, reaching out with a politely worded email shows interest and responsibility on the student's part.

Absences and Connecting to Help Each Other Recover Time Lost

It's the student's responsibility to connect with the class community and find out what she or he missed. Early in the semester, students should make acquaintance with at least one classmate, exchange contact information, and agree to share important information with each other if one is absent. It's important. Whenever students are absent for any amount of time in class, they have lost important instructional time and content.

Attending and being fully present involves making a commitment of time. Students and instructors also commit to each other—students to students, students to instructors, and instructors to students. Class is time for mutual respect, thoughtfulness, and kindness. Students should aim to build a sense of community and belonging. They should enter the classroom each day with a positive outlook. It's not always easy; sometimes it's nearly impossible. But when things are difficult, a community cares for its members. All colleges are communities filled with people and programs to help students get the assistance and guidance they need.

Absences, Deadlines, Tardies, Leaving Early

Within some academic programs or courses, even one absence may result in failing the course. In general, college students must be aware of the attendance policies (i.e., policies regarding absences, tardies, and "leaving early") indicated within each course syllabus and the college or university catalog. Double-check the syllabus for each course every semester of college. Students who know they will be absent should always contact instructors ahead of time (i.e., a month, a week, a day, or an hour before class), depending on the policies..

A missed class does not necessarily change a due date for an assignment. Students should read the course syllabus and know their instructor's policies for absences and late work. For example, if a student misses three classes without any reasonable explanations, notifications, or formal paperwork, what happens to the overall course grade? Students should know the answer after the first day of class.

Tardiness is equivalent to absence. Critically important activities often happen during the first few minutes of class, including the taking of attendance. Some instructors will count all tardies as absences and/or deduct points for each tardy.

Leaving early is the same thing as being absent. Some students mistakenly assume that "arriving" means "attending" class and that it's okay to leave class early at any time. It's not okay. Even when students think their instructors don't notice students leaving, instructors and assistants pay attention. Students not present in class could likely miss out on essential course content. However, leaving a class early may be acceptable in extenuating circumstances if a student requests permission and if the instructor approves.

Speaking of "presence," students must be physically, psychologically, and intellectually present in class each period to learn everything they possibly can.

Don't Let Electronic Devices Steal Time and Attendance

The student scrolling through websites unrelated to class content or completing homework for another course isn't completely present nor attending to task. Such students sometimes fail their courses because it's hard to truly learn without listening.; active learning occurs through notetaking and participating in class discussion—and it is helpful to turn off devices that distract and steal attention. If information about cellphones and other devices isn't in the syllabus, ask or take cues from the instructor and from other students during the first couple of days of class.

Some instructors weave the use of electronic devices into their lessons through response and polling programs, which allow students to use their devices to participate in discussions. In addition, many instructors allow and encourage the use of laptops and tablets in class, when appropriate. However, not all instructors and situations allow devices, and some instructors deduct points for cell phone use during class, so students should know the instructor's preference.

Time Communicating and Attending to Email and Learning Management Systems

Before the semester begins, students would do well to familiarize themselves with their campus email system and respective learning management system (LMS). Instructors and students use their campus LMS in a variety of ways. It's important for students to ask questions about how instructors will use the LMS and how they wish to be contacted.

The Syllabus: Words to Live By

Syllabi created for college-level courses are likely to be much longer than students have previously encountered. A course syllabus is a multiple-page document that instructors provide to students during the first few days of class. If one stays enrolled in a course, both student and instructor are expected to follow the syllabus, which usually provides the following critically important information:

- Course number, title, schedule, and final exam date and time
- Instructor's name, contact information, and office hours
- Learning Outcomes/Objectives (LOs) or goals (sometimes called Student Learning Outcomes [SLOs] or Program Learning Outcomes [PLOs], which vary amongst college and universities): Students should highlight these and keep them in mind as a checklist of goals they should meet, concepts they should learn, and skills they should demonstrate over the semester and certainly by the end of the course.
- Required materials (e.g., books, email access, computer access)
- General course tasks
- Course assignments (e.g., homework) and assessments (e.g., quizzes, exams), including formatting of written work
- Daily and/or weekly class schedule
- General course policies (e.g., attendance and participation, academic integrity, grading and late work, and suggested study times per week)
- Campus-wide support services (e.g., a writing center, learning assistance center, counseling center, health clinic, Title IX support center, and LGBTQ+ support center)
- College and university policies, rules, and guidelines

Students should read each syllabus on the first day they receive it so they are clear about all that will be expected of them for the rest of the semester.

Managing Time

It often seems the older people get, the busier their lives become. These days, increasingly more students can't complete a degree without also having to work at least one job. Add family needs into the mix, and it becomes a situation in which time can seem difficult to manage, and responsibilities in life can feel overwhelming. "Overwhelming," in fact, is a word college students often use. College is interesting, fun, exciting, and full of new ideas, and exists as a path to fulfill students' dreams, but it requires time, attention, and energy.

To feel empowered and in control of one's life, students need to proactively manage their time and life—instead of just letting life happen to them. It helps to be clear about expectations, to plan ahead, to stay organized, to anticipate any complications, and to create a schedule that works. It helps to use a planner to organize one's time. Many students benefit from creating a weekly hourly plan. Organizational strategies help maintain control over time.

Staying Organized

Some people seem more organized than others. Regardless, everyone can use strategies that work to make sure that important documents are not misplaced and that the correct essay is emailed to the correct instructor. Students should organize all their syllabi and class materials, keep up with their planners or calendars, maintain checklists of assignments and due dates, schedule study and meeting times between classes and work (i.e., actively and weekly), eat healthfully, plan for self-care (i.e., body, spirit, and mind, including sufficient sleep). Studies increasingly show the importance of sleep to a strong body, mind, and spirit, all of which affect students' ability to succeed.

Using today's technology makes staying organized easy; that's what it's there for. Calendars and software applications on cellphones can be synchronized with other devices. Online calendars can email reminders and ping cell phones so nothing is forgotten or missed.

Making Appointments with Instructors and Keeping Them

Meeting with instructors helps students obtain or process content that is significant for getting the most out of a course, but they also demonstrate a student's interest in the content and commitment to doing well in the class. Students should prepare questions beforehand and be prepared to take notes on anything the instructor offers that seems especially poignant or helpful.

If an appointment is missed, an apology is surely due. But it's important to remember that everyone misses a meeting now and then, and all one can do is apologize and try not to miss a second one.

Be Your Best Reader

Every college course will include student readings. Sometimes they're optional, but most of the time they are meant to either provide the foundation for course content or act as supplemental material. First, students discern how the course reading is meant to be accessed and used. Then, they create their own best practice including looking up, writing down, and memorizing definitions for unclear terms and finding the best places and times to read.

Close Reading

Practicing close reading can help lead toward college success. This means truly engaging with the words on the page and the content being discussed, and, most of the time, that means taking notes.

In the Inc. article "Here's How Isaac Newton Remembered Everything He Read," author Ilan Mochari explains that not only did Newton dog-ear the corners of pages in the books, he also filled the margins with words of his own . . . even if he had borrowed the book from the library (Mochari). Newton is known for his studies regarding gravity–the epiphanal moment with the falling apple. But the years of research that brought him to publish *Principia: Mathematical Principles of Natural Philosophy* in 1687 involved extensive jotting down of ideas as he crafted his genius.

These are some tips for notetaking:

- Use a variety of colored pens and highlighters and, in front of the book, a legend detailing which color represents which kind of notes.
- Take notes on a separate sheet of paper. Students should use methods that work best for them, whether using Cornell notes, informal bulleted notes, or formal outlines with Roman and Arabic numbers and letters.
- Use sticky notes. Again, using a variety of colors is great, and thoughts or questions can be written on the notes versus the pages themselves leaving the book clean thus worth more money in the buyback.

Growth Mindset

In 2007, Dr. Carol Dweck and her team of researchers studied students' attitudes about success and failure. They noticed that some students were able to deal with failure better and rebound relatively quickly while others were crushed by even the smallest of setbacks. Essentially, they determined that students who believe they can become smarter understand that making the effort can get them there. Students who believe that their intelligence is already fixed fear trying in case they prove that they aren't as smart as they think. They aren't interested in working harder. As such, Dweck coined the terms "growth mindset" and "fixed mindset" to describe how people feel about their ability to learn.

Scientists and researchers continue to study human behavior and brain activity, seeking an understanding about how and why humans succeed or fail at their endeavors, be they academic, professional, social, or even romantic. Researchers consider the way habits are formed and can be broken, the reasons for and the effects of growth versus fixed mindsets, and the role of self-discipline in achievement.

In a 2015 interview, a year after her 2014 TED talk, Dweck revisits this concept. She states, "In a growth mindset, people believe that their most basic abilities can be developed through dedication and hard work–brains and talent are just the starting point. This view creates a love of learning and a resilience that is essential for great accomplishment. . . . The key is to get students to tune in to that growth mindset (Dweck, "Carol Dweck").

The takeaway from Dweck's research and conclusions is important for all college students to consider. Where do they see themselves on the scale? They can think about ways to nurture themselves through challenging times, and reach out to instructors and anyone else who can show them how the "brains," talent, and potential for growth already exists in every individual.

Discussing with Diplomacy

During class, as a way to create meaningful discussions and extract and build knowledge, instructors often ask students to respond to questions and ideas. They may ask questions directly, with students raising their hands to politely take turns speaking. Other times, students will meet in pairs or small groups and even follow up with a whole-group discussion.

That being said, individuals have a variety of comfort zones when speaking in front of others. The fear of speaking in public is the most common fear. The following tips can help students with any level of anxiety (or comfort) during classroom discussions.

- Don't be shy. Most people feel timid. So most people empathize and are thankful someone got the discussion going.
- Don't dominate the conversation. Even if you know all the answers in class, others might too. Give everyone an equal chance to share. One good rule for an eager student to follow is to let at least two people share their ideas before jumping back in.
- Not comfortable sharing an idea? Frame it in the form of a question. Others will perceive it as sharing knowledge. This technique will actually invite further discussion and extend the conversation.

College classrooms should be safe places for learning—hostility-free and honoring open and respectful discourse.

Letters of Recommendation or Reference (LOR): Ask!

Through the course of a student's college career, many situations will arise for which the student might need a letter of recommendation (or "letter of reference"), sometimes referred to as an "LOR." Whether it be for a scholarship, an internship, study abroad, a job, or a graduate program, letters of recommendation, reference, or support are key for students and should be written by someone whom the student appreciates and trusts.

Once a student determines which instructor might be an ideal letter writer, the student should craft a formal email that includes the following elements:

- A pleasant greeting (e.g., "Good afternoon, Professor McKenna.")
- A sentence of well-wishes. (e.g., "I hope your week is moving along nicely.")
- An explanation of the email's purpose (e.g., "I'm writing to you today because I am applying for graduate school, and I would like to see if you would be willing to write a letter of recommendation for me.")
- An understanding of the instructor's busy schedule (e.g., "At this point in the semester, I am sure that you have many important responsibilities that require your time.")
- A sincere wish for their assistance (e.g., "However, if you could possibly find the time to support me with such a letter, I would be sincerely grateful.")
- A closing line (e.g., "I look forward to your response. Regardless, please know how much I have valued you as a teacher and mentor.")
- On separate lines: a pleasant closing, student's full name, course number and title, semester dates and times the student attended the professor's class (e.g., "With gratitude, Jaden Bennett, English 100, Composition I, Fall 2020, Tuesdays and Thursdays, 7:30 a.m.–8:45 a.m.")

If the instructor agrees, it's good practice to immediately send a follow up email with all important information including letter due dates and the recipient's name and address, along with any other essential information.

The letter-writer should be contacted at least one week before the letter must be received.

It's a good idea to deliver a handwritten card of thanks regardless of whether the overall results were as wished.

Works Cited

Dweck, Carol S. "Carol Dweck Revisits the 'Growth Mindset.'" *Education Week*, 23 September 2015.

Dweck, Carol S. *Mindset: The New Psychology of Success*, Random House, 2016.

Dweck, Carol S. "The Power of Believing that You Can Improve." TEDxNorrkoping, November 2014.

Mochari, Ilan. "Here's How Isaac Newton Remembered Everything He Read." *Inc.*, Manuseto Ventures, 2018.

Obama, Michelle. "Remarks by The First Lady at National Arts and Humanities Youth Program Awards." *The Obama White House Archives*, Office of the First Lady, The White House, U.S. Government, 15 November 2015 at 2:31 p.m. EST.

1.3 Intellectual Standards for Quality

The word "standard" is used to describe the level of quality that a given item possesses. So an "intellectual standard" is one that measures the overall value of a scholarly effort. Such standards apply to essays, reports, assignments, group discussions, and even notetaking. For overall success, students need to know their professors' standards and need to develop their own standards, with the concept of "intellectual standards" at the forefront.

There are nine primary intellectual standards to keep in mind: clarity, precision, accuracy, depth, breadth, logic, significance, relevance, and fairness. Keeping a list of these standards (or even using an actual checklist) and applying them to academic thinking, writing, and other scholarly interaction is an excellent way to ensure one's continued intellectual growth and college and career success.

These standards can help scholars, both students and instructors, form connected and quality ideas (e.g., "critical thinking" or "analysis") and craft written work (e.g., essays, reports, articles, reflections, and other writing sometimes known as "papers" or "homework").

Clarity: Do You Get It?

Many of the editorial comments and corrections (e.g., those from peers, mentors, tutors, and professors) shared with students regarding their written work is related to clarity. When an essay is clear, it's understandable and communicates information to readers with ease. None of the statements are confusing or ambiguous. There aren't areas within the essay where the meaning is lost due to exaggerated narrative or forced and unnatural word choice. When an essay is clear, readers can follow the path that the writer is communicating. They can read smoothly without stopping to ponder what a word or even an entire sentence means.

Sentence Clarity

Misplaced Modifiers

One way sentences become unclear is when they include misplaced (or dangling) modifiers or vague pronoun references. Here are some examples:

> Original: *The sun, as he was surfing, sparkled on the water.*

- In this sentence, the modifying phrase "as he was surfing" is placed where it modifies the sun not the surfer. (i.e., It sounds like the sun is surfing.)
- The sentence also loses clarity because the pronoun "he" is vague.

> Revised: *As Kalani surfed, the sun sparkled on the water.*

Missing Punctuation

Punctuation marks can be tricky. However, within the English language, their correct usage is essential to be sure one's intended meaning is clear. Here's an example:

Original: *Lets eat Grandma*

- ◦ Devoid of punctuation, it seems like Grandma is going to be dinner.
- ◦ To clarify, an apostrophe and a comma are needed.

Revised: *Let's eat, Grandma!*

Punctuation is for the reader, so it's important that each punctuation mark's usage is clear and that the writer knows how to use it correctly

Rhetoric: Is Meaning Clear for Everyone?

When words have more than one meaning, using them in a sentence or within an essay can pose problems related to clarity. The word "rhetoric" is one such word. Generally thought of as "the art of speaking or writing effectively," the word enters many English writing classroom discussions.

Sometimes "rhetoric" is referred to in a negative light, as in the way some people sometimes express themselves using bombastic and hyperbolic words and expressions. The Merriam-Webster dictionary also tells us that rhetoric can be defined as "the study of writing or speaking as a means of communication or persuasion" or "skill in the effective use of speech." It can even be simply considered as "verbal communication" and "discourse" ("Rhetoric," Merriam-Webster). So knowing the many definitions for this word is essential for college success because individuals, including instructors, will discuss rhetoric in a variety of ways.

The history of rhetoric is directly connected to the Greek philosopher Aristotle, whose rhetorical concepts are central for understanding the art of persuasion (also called argumentation) in both speaking and writing. Most high school students may know about logos, ethos, and pathos; however, other rhetorical concepts exist, as described below.

Clarifying Aristotelian Rhetorical Concepts

- **TELOS** is the Greek word indicating the "purpose" of a speech or text. It refers to a writer's intended purpose as well as to the audience's purpose as readers who wish to be informed by the writer's words.
- **KAIROS** translates from Greek to the "right, critical, or opportune" moment, and the term can be used when talking about the persuasion of an audience through writing or speaking. Analyzing the rhetorical techniques of a speech or text through kairos involves determining how the language within a text supports an argument using the setting, time, and place.
- **LOGOS** roughly translates to "word," and it is consistently used when determining the logic of reasoning within an argument. Some students simplify this concept to mean facts, figures, and statistics, which writers use to appeal to readers' sense of reason.
- **ETHOS** is Greek for "character," which speaks to a writer's authority and expertise. As such, incorporating ethos within an argument establishes the writer as credible. Some students simplify this concept as an "ethical appeal" or the traits of trustworthiness or credibility.

- **PATHOS** is the Greek word indicating not only "suffering" but also "experience," and it is related to feelings, beliefs, and values, sometimes simplified as an "emotional appeal." When authors use pathos as a writing technique, they are appealing to readers' emotions, beliefs, and values.
- **BATHOS** in Greek roughly means "depth," but it has evolved to address an anticlimactic situation when there is a sudden appearance of the commonplace or boring during what was otherwise serious or exciting. In modern times, the technique of bathos is often used for humorous effects in comedy, using ridiculous metaphors, figures of speech, language, and ideas.

Precision: Is It "En Pointe"?

Precision with language is critical for true understanding. For written work to be precise, it must be sufficiently detailed and what some today call "en pointe"–a term that is drawn from the realm of ballet and is French for dancing precisely on one's toes. Precision in the English language can be tricky, as English is a polyglot language (made up of multiple languages) which is fluid and constantly evolving and, like a fluid, changes shape depending on the container or context. For example, etymologists (who study words and their origins) track the term "on point"–which has become common on social media and the English vernacular–to the French "en pointe." Today, the phrase "on point" is commonly used, with few people aware of its more precise spelling and use in ballet.

Precision within writing demands that words are not only spelled correctly but that their meanings are also clear and that the words are not overused.

Punctuation needs to be used in a manner that follows standard rules, and ideas must be expressed in ways that are direct while still allowing for the writer to perform with skill and artistry.

Writing with precision at the college level entails researching, reading, and evaluating, and studying to understand information in greater detail and depth. For example, the previous explanation of rhetorical concepts is a college-level understanding that goes beyond the high-school triad of pathos, ethos, and logos, but there are more detailed and deeper readings and discussions about rhetoric in upper-level college and graduate-level courses.

Accuracy: Is It Correct? Is It True?

Accuracy is the difference between "en pointe" and "on point," between "resume" and "résumé," and between "aina" and "'āina." It's the subtleties that make all the difference. For example, English language speakers can resume (or pick up) where they left off. In French, the word "résumé" is a short, employment-related document detailing one's education, work history, and job and people skills.

But today, the French meaning has become part of the English vernacular, and the accent marks are often omitted while the word retains its dual meaning. Using older technology, writers sometimes were unable to include the French accent marks. Today, software often automatically will add them for precise, accurate spelling.

In Hawai'i, the popular expression "mālama āina" encourages people to take care of the earth. Because the Hawaiian alphabet includes the glottal stop (or 'okina ['], a consonant) and long vowels indicated by the macron (or kahakō, the line above long vowels), omitting or changing the letters of the alphabet changes the meanings of words just as they do in English (e.g., "red," "read," and "bed" have different meanings based on letters used or omitted).

Accuracy in spelling in any language is essential. For example, in Hawaiian, the word "'āina" (with the 'okina and kahakō for the long ā) means "land," but "'aina" (with just the initial 'okina) means "meal" (among other things), and "aina" (without either of the marks necessary to accurately form two of the Hawaiian alphabets) means "sexual intercourse." The glottal stop and the macron are important marks forming complete letters within the Hawaiian alphabet, just as any English word relies on every necessary marking (as in the line that forms a "t" and, if omitted is an "l" or the number "one"). Clearly, accuracy is important across the world's languages.

As scholars and writers across the world become more globally aware, they grow more accurate in the use of others' languages. Students who are developing their expertise and college success skills also grow more aware of the importance of accuracy, not only when it comes to spelling, punctuation, and word usage, but also grammar, syntax, and conducting research within and outside of their respective disciplines.

Depth: Is It Sufficiently Complex?

When writing or speech is deep, it covers the complexity of a topic. It doesn't skim the surface. It dives deeply into the profound knowledge and substantial understanding of a topic. For example, a list explaining rhetoric as made up of three concepts (logos, ethos, and pathos) is not as deep and complex as a list showing six concepts (the three plus bathos, telos, and kairos) or even longer lists with deeper descriptions and definitions. In another example, students progress from one-page book reports in elementary school to deeper, comparative, and analytical essays in college.

When analyzing the depth of any essay, including their own essays and those of their peers, students can ask these types of questions:

- How deeply does this essay go into its topic?
- Is it detailed enough?
- Did it go far enough into the research and reviews of other texts to demonstrate a deep knowledge about the subject?
- How thoroughly have specific subtopics within a major been researched?

Breadth: Are All Views Considered?

Breadth is how broad or wide a topic has been discussed in writing or in speech. For example, to attain breadth in a persuasive essay, a writer must consider not only one point of view, but all the multiple major perspectives about an issue. Breadth also entails considering multiple contexts of an issue and multiple analytical approaches to solving a problem.

Breadth means reading more than a handful of articles supporting one side of an issue; it means reading more articles supporting various perspectives so the writer can truly understand all viewpoints about the issue and can discuss the issue with breadth that builds a deeper understanding and fairness. When analyzing the breadth of any essay, students and instructors ask questions such as the following:

- Is the content of an essay sufficiently comprehensive enough to cover a wide range of perspectives and angles on a given topic?
- Is anything missing that should be included in the scope of the topic and which would help the essay achieve enough breadth?
- Has the opposing view (i.e., the "naysayer's" perspective) been explored so as to strengthen the writer's own

argument? (This consideration is particularly key in the development of a fully supported and wisely composed persuasive or argumentative essay.)

- What has not yet been considered to make this idea or essay complete?

Logic: Does It All Make Sense?

For students to create valid arguments through essays or other written works that are meant to be persuasive, they must use accurate reasoning and avoid logical fallacies. Fallacies are arguments that use faulty reasoning, thus making them illogical. If text makes a reader stop and think, "Wait. What?" it may mean the writer needs to work on logic.

Logic exists as the essence of philosophy, mathematics, computer programming, computer science, and most other science and technology disciplines. It requires step-by-step thinking and progression in order to design a machine that works or to research and write a report worthy of submission for potential publication.

When analyzing the logic of any text, students and instructors ask questions such as the following:

- Does a sentence, paragraph, or argument make sense?
- Does one point follow another point with reason and connected ideas and transitions, rather than jumping from point A to point Z without sufficient explanation of how they are related?
- Are all assertions fortified by sufficient evidence?
- Does all data collected, whether determined as relevant or not, follow a logical approach?

Significance: Does It Matter?

The intellectual standard of significance indicates the importance and weight of a topic or point and is connected to logic and depth. For example, the deeper, broader definition of "rhetoric" from the Aristotelian perspective is more significant than the everyday, newspaper use of the word.

Significance is related to the level of importance of one thing in relation to the grander scheme of things and to the additional standards of priority and value. For example, students might write about an 18-year-old person's right to drink alcohol, but that essay would be less significant than essays about increased drunk-driving-related fatalities in the community. Some 18 year olds might argue that, if they can be drafted into the military and be required to go to war, they should have the right to drink. However, the other side of the argument asserts the right of people of all ages to travel safely on the roads, and holding back on allowing hundreds more individuals from potentially driving drunk has more weight.

When analyzing the significance of any document, students and instructors ask questions such as the following:

- Is the information important enough to include?
- Does the information answer the question asked in an assignment?
- What key points are most important for writers to include and for readers to consider?
- Is this topic important in relation to other topics in the same subject area?
- What's the most important thing to focus on?
- Is this topic worth the writer's time researching and the reader's time reading?
- Would there be enough readers interested in this topic?
- So what? Why is a topic or point more important than another topic or point?

Relevance: Is It Essential to the Main Idea?

If paragraphs in an essay are relevant, they are related to the main topic and help support the main idea with additional, related, relevant details and evidence. If paragraphs are irrelevant, a reader might think, "Wait. What? How is this on topic?"

If, for example, an essay begins by stating that government officials should take five major actions to solve the issue of homelessness in Hawai'i, but then the majority of the body paragraphs wander into opinions focused on the history of governmental decision-making in the islands for decades, a reader might feel lost and wonder how much of the content of the essay is related to solving homelessness in Hawai'i.

When analyzing the relevance of any essay, students and instructors ask questions such as the following:

- Does this point help readers understand the main issue?
- Does this essay focus on the assignment question or prompt?
- Does it answer the main question?
- If this paragraph is slightly off-topic, what can be done to refocus it so that it does its job in supporting the main idea in the thesis statement?
- If a point is confusing readers who don't understand how it's related to the main idea, does it belong in this essay?

Fairness: Is It Objective and Judicious?

The word "fair" is often used synonymously with "just" or "judicious" and is related to "justice." Especially in essays that are meant to persuade through logical argumentation, topics and points of view (POVs or "perspectives") need to be treated fairly and diplomatically. A fair, even-handed treatment doesn't necessarily mean agreeing to opposing (or "naysayer's") POVs, but strong, college-level writing must acknowledge the opposing POVs, then must either accommodate or refute them. For example, an essay may state, "The opponents have valid points regarding X and Y. They are right about this and that. However, they are innaccurate about this specific point about X, and their argument doesn't negate A and B, which remains the most accurate ideas and still strongly support this argument."

When analyzing the fairness of any essay, students and instructors ask questions such as the following:

- Does the writer of this essay exhibit the ability to fairly assess the viewpoints of others, even opposing viewpoints?
- Are there any fallacies, such as ad hominems that unfairly label opponents rather than speak directly and precisely about the opposing argument or POV itself? (Note: The term "ad hominem" is Short for "argumentum ad hominem" and is a fallacious argumentative strategy whereby genuine discussion of the topic at hand is avoided by instead attacking the character, motive, or other attribute of the person making the argument, or persons associated with the argument, rather than attacking the substance of the argument itself.)
- Does the writer or speaker have a conflict of interest? Does that conflict of interest appear as bias in the text? Given today's political scene and questionable statements by government officials, this question may bear more significance.

Apply the Intellectual Standards to Studying and Writing

Students and instructors in colleges and the universities often consider the quality of their own and others' work by applying the concepts of intellectual standards, whether or not they are aware of them or have had them articulated for them. Scholarship is evaluated for quality in terms of clarity, precision, accuracy, depth, breadth, logic, significance, relevance, and fairness. Successful college-level studying involves reading, annotating, writing, discussing, and analyzing information and involves practicing skills to apply new knowledge, all of which result in learning and building expertise. Writing to communicate, writing to learn, and writing to demonstrate learning and skills are key skills in college and should demonstrate the mindful application of intellectual standards.

Activities

1. View and take notes on the video "The Intellectual Standards: An Introduction," posted by Gary Meegan on April 2, 2014. Review the notes. Then describe and define the nine intellectual standards, using your own (and different and unique) words and phrasing. Then use the nine intellectual standards to evaluate a partner's personalized descriptions.
2. View the video "Shot on iPhone XS–Don't mess with Mother–Apple," posted by the Apple company. Take notes on observations about the visual and audio rhetoric and observations on what the images, movements, music, and words communicate, how they meet intellectual standards, and how they meet the company's purpose(s) for creating the video.

Works Cited

Apple. "Shot on iPhone XS – Don't mess with Mother – Apple." *YouTube*, 17 April 2019.

Meegan, Gary. "The Intellectual Standards: An Introduction." *YouTube*, 2 April 2014.

"Rhetoric." *Meriam–Webster Online*. Merriam-Webster, LLC.

Additional Resources

Elder, Linda, and Richard Paul. "Universal Intellectual Standards." *The Foundation for Critical Thinking*, October 2010.

Foundation for Critical Thinking at CriticalThinking.org.

Hill, David Jayne. "*Bathos.*" *The Elements of Rhetoric and Composition: A Text-book for Schools and Colleges.* Sheldon, 1878.

Paul, Richard, and Linda Elder. "Critical Thinking: Intellectual Standards Essential to Reasoning Within Every Domain of Human Thought, Part Two." *Journal of Developmental Education*, Volume 37, Issue 1, Fall 2013, pp. 32-36.

Rapp, Christof. "Aristotle's Rhetoric." *The Stanford Encyclopedia of Philosophy* (Spring 2010 Edition), Edward N. Zalta (ed.)

Smith, Robin. "Aristotle's Logic." *The Stanford Encyclopedia of Philosophy* (Summer 2019 Edition), Edward N. Zalta (ed.), [forthcoming]

CHAPTER 2. THE WRITING PROCESS

2.1 Introduction

Photo by Debby Hudson on Unsplash

Learning Objectives

The student will be able to do the following:

- Use prewriting to prepare to write a well-developed college essay.
- Strategically draft, revise, and edit an effective college essay appropriate to the audience and purpose of the assignment.

A Student's Story

When Kiana started taking college classes, she brought with her a belief that she was not a very strong writer. This lack of confidence was, unfortunately, developed throughout her K-12 education. In elementary school, she struggled with spelling. In middle school, she found that her vocabulary were embarrassingly limited. In high school, she struggled with what she thought must be writer's block, sitting down to finally write a draft right before it was due, and finding that she could only produce a paragraph before feeling like she had nothing else to say.

As she entered college and enrolled in her first-year writing course, she was anxious about attending a required conference with her instructor, who was meeting with each student to discuss the rough drafts of their first essays. She handed her draft to her instructor knowing that it was far from the required length. Before reading it, he asked her about the process that she had used to write it. Kiana confessed that she had worked on it just the night before.

"Did you do any prewriting?" he asked.

"No," she said. "I just sat down and wrote this."

When Kiana was asked to read her essay aloud, several issues became evident. The overall purpose of her essay was unclear, and the narrative rambled making many points but not developing any of them. The narrative lacked detail in some parts and had too much information in other parts. Throughout the composition, Kiana heard words and phrases that were completely repetitive, and she also used some words awkwardly because she had searched for synonyms that didn't actually work within the context of the sentence.

When she finished reading, her instructor suggested that she avoid directly working on that draft until she had done some prewriting activities that would help her organize her ideas, develop her thesis, and refine and develop her content.

"Don't worry yet about spelling and word choice. First, you need to explore and identify your ideas. Here are some fun, helpful exercises that will help you to do that efficiently. Then, when you come back to drafting, you'll find it goes more quickly. Worry about the mechanics such as your grammar and punctuation after you've written a draft that says what you want to say."

Kiana went home feeling better about getting back on her computer to work on her essay. Once Kiana learned the value of prewriting, drafting, and revision techniques as parts of the writing process, she started to enjoy the writing process a bit more. She was able to avoid the feeling of writer's block, and she found herself feeling more confident as a writer and better able to produce essays that she was proud to submit to her instructors.

2.2 Prewriting

Prewriting is an essential activity for most writers. Through robust prewriting, writers generate ideas, explore directions, and find their way into their writing. When students attempt to write an essay without developing their ideas, strategizing their desired structure, and focusing on precision with words and phrases, they can end up with a "premature draft"–one that is more writer-based than reader-based and, thus, might not be received by readers in the way the writer intended.

In addition, a lack of prewriting can cause students to experience writer's block. Writer's block is the feeling of being stuck when faced with a writing task. It is often caused by fear, anxiety, or a tendency toward perfectionism, but it can be overcome through prewriting activities that allow writers to relax, catch their breath, gather ideas, and gain momentum.

The following exist as the goals of prewriting:

- Contemplating the many possible ideas worth writing about.
- Developing ideas through brainstorming, freewriting, and focused writing.
- Planning the structure of the essay overall so as to have a solid introduction, meaningful body paragraphs, and a purposeful conclusion.

Discovering and Developing Ideas

Quick Prewriting Activities

Quick strategies for developing ideas include brainstorming, freewriting, and focused writing. These activities are done quickly, with a sense of freedom, while writers silence their inner critic. In her book *Wild Mind*, teacher and writer Natalie Goldberg describes this freedom as the "creator hand" freely allowing thoughts to flow onto the page while the "editor hand" remains silent. Sometimes, these techniques are done in a timed situation (usually two to ten minutes), which allows writers to get through the shallow thoughts and dive deeper to access the depths of the mind.

Brainstorming begins with writing down or typing a few words and then filling the page with words and ideas that are related or that seem important without allowing the inner critic to tell the writer if these ideas are acceptable or not. Writers do this quickly and without too much contemplation. Students will know when they are succeeding because the lists are made without stopping.

Freewriting is the "most effective way" to improve one's writing, according to Peter Elbow, the educator and writer who first coined the term "freewriting" in pivotal book *Writing Without Teachers*, published in 1973. Freewriting is a great technique for loosening up the writing muscle. To freewrite, writers must silence the inner critic and the "editor hand" and allow the "creator hand" a specified amount of time (usually from 10 to 20 minutes) to write nonstop about whatever comes to mind. The goal is to keep the hand moving, the mind contemplating, and the individual writing. If writers feel stuck, they just keep writing "I don't know what to write" until new ideas form and develop in the mind and flow onto the page.

Focused freewriting entails writing freely–and without stopping, during a limited time–about a specific topic. Once writers are relaxed and exploring freely, they may be surprised about the ideas that emerge.

Researching

Unlike quick prewriting activities, researching is best done slowly and methodically and, depending on the project, can take a considerable amount of time. Researching is exciting, as students activate their curiosity and learn about the topic, developing ideas about the direction of their writing. The goal of researching is to gain background understanding on a topic and to check one's original ideas against those of experts. However, it is important for the writer to be aware that the process of conducting research can become a trap for procrastinators. Students often feel like researching a topic is the same as doing the assignment, but it's not.

The two aspects of researching that are often misunderstood are as follows:

1. Writers start the research process too late so the information they find never really becomes their own setting themselves up for way more quoting, paraphrasing, and summarizing the words of others than is appropriate for the 70% one's own words and 30% the words of others ratio necessary for college-level research-based writing.
2. Writers become so involved in the research process that they don't start the actual writing process soon enough so as to meet a due date with a well written, edited, and revised finished composition.

Being thoughtful about limiting one's research time—and using a planner of some sort to organize one's schedule—is a way to keep oneself from starting the research process too late to

See Part V of this book for more information about researching.

Audience and Purpose

It's important that writers identify the audience and the purpose of a piece of writing. To whom is the writer communicating? Why is the writer writing? Students often say they are writing for whomever is grading their work at the end. However, most students will be sharing their writing with peers and reviewers (e.g., writing tutors, peer mentors). The audience of any piece of college writing is, at the very minimum, the class as a whole. As such, it's important for the writer to consider the expertise of the readers, which includes their peers and professors). There are even broader applications. For example, students could even send their college writing to a newspaper or a legislator, or share it online for the purpose of informing or persuading decision-makers to make changes to improve the community. Good writers know their audience and maintain a purpose to mindfully help and intentionally shape their essays for meaning and impact. Students should think beyond their classroom and about how their writing could have an impact on their campus community, their neighborhood, and the wider world.

Planning the Structure of an Essay

Planning Based on Audience and Purpose

Identifying the target audience and purpose of an essay is a critical part of planning the structure and techniques that are best to use. It's important to consider the following:

- Is the the purpose of the essay to educate, announce, entertain, or persuade?

- Who might be interested in the topic of the essay?
- Who would be impacted by the essay or the information within it?
- What does the reader know about this topic?
- What does the reader need to know in order to understand the essay's points?
- What kind of hook is necessary to engage the readers and their interest?
- What level of language is required? Words that are too subject-specific may make the writing difficult to grasp for readers unfamiliar with the topic.
- What is an appropriate tone for the topic? A humorous tone that is suitable for an autobiographical, narrative essay may not work for a more serious, persuasive essay.

Hint: Answers to these questions help the writer to make clear decisions about diction (i.e., the choice of words and phrases), form and organization, and the content of the essay.

Use Audience and Purpose to Plan Language

In many classrooms, students may encounter the concept of language in terms of correct versus incorrect. However, this text approaches language from the perspective of appropriateness. Writers should consider that there are different types of communities, each of which may have different perspectives about what is "appropriate language" and each of which may follow different rules, as John Swales discussed in "The Concept of Discourse Community." Essentially, Swales defines discourse communities as "groups that have goals or purposes, and use communication to achieve these goals."

Writers (and readers) may be more familiar with a home community that uses a different language than the language valued by the academic community. For example, many people in Hawai'i speak Hawai'i Creole English (HCE colloquially regarded as "Pidgin"), which is different from academic English. This does not mean that one language is better than another or that one community is homogeneous in terms of language use; most people "code-switch" from one "code" (i.e., language or way of speaking) to another. It helps writers to be aware and to use an intersectional lens to understand that while a community may value certain language practices, there are several types of language practices within our community.

What language practices does the academic discourse community value? The goal of first-year-writing courses is to prepare students to write according to the conventions of academia and Standard American English (SAE). Understanding and adhering to the rules of a different discourse community does not mean that students need to replace or drop their own discourse. They may add to their language repertoire as education continues to transform their experiences with language, both spoken and written. In addition to the linguistic abilities they already possess, they should enhance their academic writing skills for personal growth in order to meet the demands of the working world and to enrich the various communities they belong to.

Use Techniques to Plan Structure

Before writing a first draft, writers find it helpful to begin organizing their ideas into chunks so that they (and readers) can efficiently follow the points as organized in an essay.

First, it's important to decide whether to organize an essay (or even just a paragraph) according to one of the following:

- Chronological order (organized by time)

- Spatial order (organized by physical space from one end to the other)
- Prioritized order (organized by order of importance)

There are many ways to plan an essay's overall structure, including mapping and outlining.

Mapping (which sometimes includes using a graphic organizer) involves organizing the relationships between the topic and other ideas. The following is example (from ReadWriteThink.org, 2013) of a graphic organizer that could be used to write a basic, persuasive essay:

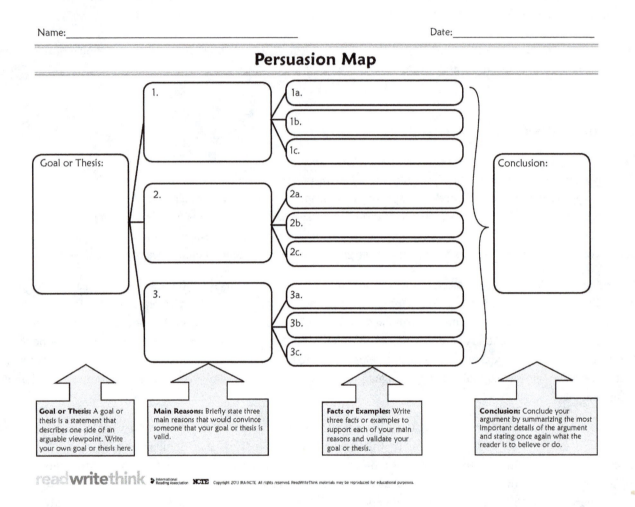

Persuasion Map. Copyright 2013 IRA/NCTE. All rights reserved. ReadWriteThink materials may be reproduced for educational purposes.

Outlining is also an excellent way to plan how to organize an essay. Formal outlines use levels of notes, with Roman numerals for the top level, followed by capital letters, Arabic numerals, and lowercase letters. Here's an example:

I. Introduction

    A. Hook/Lead/Opener: According to the Leilani was shocked when a letter from Chicago said her "Aloha Poke" restaurant was infringing on a non-Hawaiian Midwest restaurant that had trademarked the words "aloha" (the Hawaiian word for love, compassion, mercy, and other things besides serving as a greeting) and "poke" (a Hawaiian dish of raw fish and seasonings).

B. Background information about trademarks, the idea of language as property, the idea of cultural identity, and the question about who owns language and whether it can be owned.

C. Thesis Statement (with the main point and previewing key or supporting points that become the topic sentences of the body paragraphs): While some business people use language and trademarks to turn a profit, the nation should consider that language cannot be owned by any one group or individual and that former (or current) imperialist and colonialist nations must consider the impact of their actions on culture and people groups, and legislators should bar the trademarking of non-English words for the good of internal peace of the country.

II. Body Paragraphs

A. Main Point (Topic Sentence): Some business practices involve co-opting languages for the purpose of profit.

1. Supporting Detail 1: Information from Book 1—Supporting Sentences

a. Subpoint

2. Supporting Detail 2: Information from Article 1—Supporting Sentences

a. Subpoint

b. Subpoint

B. Main Point (Topic Sentence): Language cannot be owned by any one group or individual.

1. Supporting Detail 1: Information from Book 1—Supporting Sentences

a. Subpoint

2. Supporting Detail 2: Information from Article 1—Supporting Sentences

a. Subpoint

b. Subpoint

C. Main Point (Topic Sentence): Once (or currently) imperialist and colonialist nations must consider the impact of their actions on culture and people groups.

1. Supporting Detail

a. Subpoint

D. Legislators should bar the trademarking of non-English words for the good and internal peace of the country.

III. Conclusion (Revisit the Hook/Lead/Opener, Restate the Thesis, End with a Twist—a strong more globalized statement about why this topic was important to write about)

Note about outlines: Informal outlines can be created using lists with or without bullets. What is important is that main and subpoint ideas are linked and identified.

Activities

1. Use 10 minutes to freewrite with the goal to "empty your cup"—writing about whatever is on your mind or blocking your attention on your classes, job, or family. This can be a great way to help you become centered, calm, or focused, especially when dealing with emotional challenges in your life.

2. For each writing assignment in class, spend three 10-minute sessions either listing (brainstorming) or focused-writing about the topic before starting to organize and outline key ideas.

3. Before each draft or revision of assignments, spend 10 minutes focused-writing an introduction and a

thesis statement that lists all the key points that supports the thesis statement.

4. Have a discussion in your class about the various language communities that you and your classmates experience in your town or on your island.
5. Create a graphic organizer that will help you write various types of essays.
6. Create a metacognitive, self-reflective journal: Freewrite continuously (e.g., 5 times a week, for at least 10 minutes, at least half a page) about what you learned in class or during study time. Document how your used your study hours this week, how it felt to write in class and out of class, what you learned about writing and about yourself as a writer, how you saw yourself learning and evolving as a writer, what you learned about specific topics. What goals do you have for the next week?

During the second half of the semester, as you begin to tackle deeper and lengthier assignments, the journal should grow to at least one page per day, at least 20 minutes per day, as you use journal writing to reflect on writing strategies (e.g., structure, organization, rhetorical modes, research, incorporating different sources without plagiarizing, giving and receiving feedback, planning and securing time in your schedule for each task involved in a writing assignment) and your ideas about topics, answering research questions, and reflecting on what you found during research and during discussions with peers, mentors, tutors, and instructors. The journal then becomes a record of your journey as a writer, as well as a source of freewriting on content that you can shape into paragraphs for your various assignments.

Works Cited

Elbow, Peter. *Writing Without Teachers*. 2nd edition, 1973, Oxford UP, 1998.

Goldberg, Natalie. *Wild Mind : Living the Writer's Life*. Bantam Books, 1990.

Swales, John. "The Concept of Discourse Community." *Genre Analysis: English in Academic and Research Settings*, 1990, pp. 21-32.

For more about discourse communities, see the online class by Robert Mohrenne "What is a Discourse Community?" ENC 1102 13 Fall 0027. University of Central Florida, 2013.

2.3 Drafting

Once students have spent time and effort preparing to write by gathering ideas and organizing activities, they are ready to begin drafting. Many instructors recommend a practice that is referred to as fast drafting, in which the student writes under the pressure of a time limit, much like freewriting. This allows students to create without their inner critic undermining their momentum. It empowers the "creator hand" to work with agency, while silencing the "editor hand."

To do fast drafting, students first need to set up the conditions that will help in their success and is appropriate to their abilities to focus. The following are easy steps writers follow:

- Create a block of time in which there are no interruptions. This should be a realistic length, given a writer's ability to focus, from 10 minutes at a time to 75 minutes or longer.
- Decide on the goal: Write a paragraph in 10 minutes, 2 pages in 1 hour, or a complete essay in 1 hour and 15 minutes.

For some, 75 minutes is a good length, but some students find that after 30 minutes they can no longer concentrate. If that is the case, they should plan on several shorter sessions of distraction-free time.

During this time, students should turn off their phones and social media, let the dog outside, and ensure that it's time for children to be asleep. This needs to be quiet, concentrated time.

Students need to let go of their worries about good and bad ideas. There will be time to rethink, rephrase, and rework during the revision process.

Activities

Prepare for writing a 75-minute fast draft by doing several prewriting activities including brainstorming, focused writing, outlining, and perhaps reading and researching, depending on the assignment. Then, in an intense, 75-minute time span, write your entire essay as quickly as possible including the introduction and conclusion. Don't stop to concern yourself with word choice, citations, or grammar. Just get into the flow of ideas and write your essay all the way to the end. Remember: You can go back and revise and edit all you want, but that is much easier to do once you have a draft.

2.4 Revision

The Revision Process

Revision literally means to re-see or re-envision a piece of writing. This process may involve adding, rearranging, removing, and replacing (ARRR) words, sentences, and ideas. Since writing is recursive, revising may require revisiting the prewriting stage.

- **A**dding

    What else does the reader need to know? If the essay doesn't meet the required word or page count, what areas can be expanded? Where would further explanation help key points to be more clear? This is a good time to go back to the prewriting notes and look for ideas which weren't included in the draft.

- **R**earranging

    Even when writers carefully plan their writing, they may need to rearrange sections for their essays to flow better.

- **R**emoving

    Some ideas just don't work or don't contribute enough to the overall goal of the essay. Often when writers delete excess words or paragraphs, the ideas become clearer.

- **R**eplacing

    Vivid details help bring writing to life. Writers need to look for strong examples and quotable passages from outside sources to support their arguments. If particular paragraphs aren't working well, writers need to try rewriting them.

Other Useful Strategies

- **Reverse Outlining**

    In reverse outlining, the student reads through the written text and notes, noting down the topic of each paragraph. This way, the student can review if each paragraph has a clear focus and if each paragraph fits the overall organization of the paper. More on reverse outlining is available at *The Purdue Online Writing Lab* (OWL), "Reverse Outlining: An Exercise for Taking Notes and Revising Your Work."

- **Reading Aloud**

    The act of reading one's essay aloud allows the student to "hear it" in the way a reader will. This act permits the writer to slow down and pay attention to all words in the essay. They get a sense of what a reader experiences, where words are clear and effective, and where they are weak. Poorly structured sentences are hard to read out loud, indicating that this would be a good place to start revising. This technique is a great precursor for receiving feedback from others. It also helps writers take responsibility for their writing.

- **Peer and Instructor Feedback**

  No one becomes a good writer in a vacuum. Sometimes writing is done for ourselves, but more often, writing is done to connect to others, to share thoughts, and to communicate something others need to know. At this stage of the process, it's important for writers to get the measure of how well their writing works for readers that they are wanting to entertain, educate, or persuade. Showing the writing to someone else is essential. This might be done in a writers' circle or just with a friend who is good with words and can be asked for feedback. It's best to show our work to several people to get more than one opinion. Receiving feedback helps writers discover the strengths in their writing as well as areas that may be improved.

  After receiving feedback, whether through track changes in Google Docs, Microsoft Word, on paper, or verbally in a peer-review session, the writer can discuss the comments with the reviewer. It's important that a writer consider these comments. Every reader comes from a different point of view, and the writer may not agree with everything that gets said by various readers. Sometimes, comments will be contradictory. It is the writer's responsibility to ask further and decide how to use comments received. A community that embraces and nurtures its members through the revision process works to communicate feedback so that everyone can grow and learn.

  Successful college students utilize their resources, specifically their instructors and peers, to get feedback. Tutoring is an effective means by which students can receive knowledgeable one-on-one feedback about their writing. It can also be an effective way to help manage time.

  Peer mentors provide students with additional one-on-one and group support in writing classrooms or during office hours. The peer mentor has had the previous experience of completing similar writing assignments and students find it helpful when they revise with their expertise in mind.

Activities

1. Take an essay that you have written under time pressure. Create a reverse outline of the different sections of your text. Observe whether this outline makes sense. Try moving around the different parts of your essay. Are there structures that help you to highlight certain ideas or make them more powerful?
2. Find a partner or group of classmates who are willing to meet at least once a week. During your meetings, read your essays aloud and give each other feedback on the content and language of your essays. This should be a group you are committed to working with throughout the semester with the goal of helping each other grow as writers.
3. Make an appointment with your instructor or college tutor to work through prewriting, revising or editing stages of your writing process.

2.5 Editing

The process of editing is an ongoing activity for all writers. From the time they come up with a possible topic, they begin editing their ideas and directions in which to go. Once they begin to write, however, the editing takes a new path. Writers edit their own work by reading with fresh eyes and deciding if words need to be moved around or changed. They look for misspellings and awkward wording, and they rework for the sake of clarity. They ask themselves, "Is this saying what I think it does? Am I being as clear as possible? Is there a more concise or artful way that I can express this important idea?" They check their work for typos and unintentional repetition of words and phrases, and they check all the grammar, spelling, capitalization, and punctuation.

However, it is extremely important not to focus on editing too early in the writing process. If a student writes one sentence or paragraph and immediately begins to edit it, they may find that they lose the flow of their ideas. Suddenly, while focusing on how to spell a word, the whole rest of the essay gets put on hold. The inner editor or critic can inhibit writers, causing them to lose flow and to experience perfectionism and writer's block. Most instructors recommend that writers ban their critics until they have completed their first drafts and revision has taken place. This saves writers the wasted effort that comes with closely editing material that doesn't make the final cut anyway.

At later points during the document's creation, an outside set of editorial eyes may be needed–those of a peer, instructor, colleague, or formal editor–to help move that piece of text toward excellence. In addition to the big-picture structural or information-based considerations, the need for a comma or better word may be the focus of editing efforts. Good editing allows the writer to submit the written creation with the confidence that it is the best it can be and stands as something to truly be proud of.

Grammar: The Grand Dame

According to Merriam-Webster, grammar is a system of rules that defines the structure of a language. For most of the USA, that system is Standard American English (SAE). Grammar is the way people use language rules and how words are used in a certain order to form phrases and clauses that relay a meaning for readers. The term "syntax" (the art of sentence structure) goes hand-in-hand with this.

Writers and speakers of any given language are aware that the rules related to grammar and usage of that language are largely appropriated not by formal instruction and memorization but informally and even subconsciously as one grows up listening, speaking and reading. So it's important to note that, as those who use language every day, students already have internalized essential grammar rules. Most college writers struggle with only one or two main grammar blind-spots, like how to correctly use a comma or semicolon. Once they master these, they can confidently edit their own work.

Language Usage

Writing is all about decision-making. Writers need to ask, "How should I craft this sentence, this paragraph? Given the effect of two possible punctuation marks, which one should I use? What is the effect of this word instead of that one, so similar in meaning but carrying a more negative connotation?" In this way, writing is about making endless choices.

Precision of Words

Sometimes, in early drafting, writers fall back on words that are vague or boring. For example, consider sentences starting with "This" or "It." Unless the previous sentence made it totally clear what the "This" or the "It" is, the reader will be confused. For example,

Instead of the following: "This is an exciting point in the movie."

How about this?

"The surprise ending of movie is exciting."

The same thing goes for starting a sentence with the personal pronoun "It." See the two sentences below.

Instead of this: "It caused the audience to break into applause."

Define the "It" like this. "The final scene caused the audience to break into applause."

To note, this kind of sentence structure is essentially using words as "filler" to take up space within a sentence and creates a sort of vagueness for the reader who will wonder what the subject of the sentence might be. Sometimes such sentence construction is fine, but writers use it too often.

In addition, many students believe that using one of the following words adds an element of description or accentuation to their phrases; however, these specific words are overused by writers and should be given special consideration:

- Really
- Very
- Just

Trick #1: If writers conduct a global search for each of the three words above, they can use them as "red flags" to alert themselves to the perfect place to try to find a better way of saying what they want to say. How does one improve vocabulary? Use a thesaurus and read more.

What's a word for "very scary"? Frightening.

What's another way of saying "really hungry"? Famished.

On another note: The phrase "a lot" has generally outrun it's usage by the time one reaches college. Generalizations are better avoided, as they are vague and imprecise. Academics prefer statistics and specific, verifiable statements.

Repetition of Words and Phrases

The unintentional repetition of words and phrases is one of the most common oversights writers make. They all have their go-to words—ones that come naturally to them when they speak and write. The general advice is for writers to use a thesaurus to find a synonym for the overused word. However, what if there isn't a synonym for the word? Look at the paragraph below:

> This past summer, I had the opportunity to intern at Sea Life Park. Sea Life Park is known for being an exciting destination for locals and tourists to experience the wonders of sea life from throughout the Pacific. At the park, green sea turtles, or Honu, thrive and even continue to have babies. In addition, dolphins and the Hawaiian monk

seals provide visitors with the ability to view these majestic creatures but also learn about their significance within the Pacific Ocean ecosystem and their importance within island culture.

This writer's paragraph isn't bad. However, "Sea Life Park" is repeated twice in the first two sentences. In addition, in sentence three, he begins with "At the park" followed by another "sea." He defended his construction and word choice by stating, "But there isn't another word for 'Sea Life Park.'" Indeed, the "find a synonym" strategy would not work in this case just like there isn't a synonym for "parking lot" or "ice cream sundae." So another trick has to be used.

Trick #2: If a synonym doesn't exist, remove the repetitive words and combine the sentences.

> This past summer, I had the opportunity to intern at Sea Life Park, known for being an exciting destination for locals and tourists to experience the wonders of sea life from throughout the Pacific.

Replacing the repeated phrase with a comma before "known" does the trick. But wait. The phrase "sea life" appears again a little later in this same sentence. Now what?

Trick #3: Use your creativity to craft an original way of saying the same thing. Instead of "Sea Life Park," call it "the world-renowned marine playground committed to protection, preservation, and education" and the writer has not only fixed the repetition issue but also introduced wonderfully original prose.

Trick #4: Writers should read everything out loud so the ear can catch what the eye might miss.

Voice, for writers, is something uniquely their own. It's the way they put words together and involves their distinctive way of looking at the world. It makes one writer's work stand out from that of others in its originality and authenticity. Key, though, is understanding that the development of one's writing voice takes time and is ever changing. That's what makes it so exciting.

Here are samples of sentences from two famous writers. Though both these writers lived in America at approximately the same time, their "voices" are very different. What are the elements that make these sentences so different?

> It was very late and everyone had left the cafe except an old man who sat in the shadow the leaves of the tree made against the electric light. In the daytime the street was dusty, but at night the dew settled the dust and the old man liked to sit late because he was deaf and now at night it was quiet and he felt the difference. (Ernest Hemingway, "A Clean, Well-Lighted Place.")

> Alive, Miss Emily had been a tradition, a duty, and a care, a sort of hereditary obligation upon the town, dating from that day in 1894 when Colonel Sartoris, the mayor—he who fathered the edict that no woman should appear on the streets without an apron—remitted her taxes, the dispensation dating from the death of her father on into perpetuity. (William Faulkner, "A Rose for Emily.")

Style: Style is much broader than voice. Some writers have a writing style that's complex and packed with personification, metaphor, and imagery. Other writers have a more straightforward style with more simplicity or directness.

Engaging the Reader

When it comes down to it, writers within the academic setting do best when they acknowledge that what they are trying to produce is reader-based prose—written content that informs the reader of the essential message the writer is wanting to convey and also does so in a manner that is engaging and well-received.

On this note, it is important that the reader is able to follow the path of words, images, and meaning that the writer is wanting to create. Readers can become distracted and disinterested by awkward word choices, unintentional repetition, and incorrect spelling, grammar, word usage, and punctuation.

Spelling

All writers have words that give them hassles, even if they have learned how to spell those words. Does the word "essence" end with a "ce" or "se"? Does the word "privilege" spend any time on the "ledge"?

By the time one reaches college, one knows if spelling words correctly comes easily or not. And everyone knows that spell-checkers won't pick up every mistake. Writers need to make time for careful editing and proofreading throughout the writing process with an extra special proofreading session before turning in any assignment. In addition, though, here is a trick that can actually help one become a better speller, even into adulthood.

Trick #5: Create a running list of all the words that you tend to misspell. If you find another word, add it to the list. Every time you sit down to write, scroll through your list. You'll find that the spelling will become less of an issue.

Punctuation and Mechanics

Punctuation refers to the "symbols" writers use to help readers understand and process the information they wish to convey through the sentences they write. Somewhat like the notes and rests within a piece of music help musicians move quickly or slowly through a composition, punctuation marks are used for effect.

Mechanics are established rules within a language system, and sometimes include the individual decisions writers make regarding the use of capitalization, underlining, italicizing, numbers versus numerals, the placement of specific punctuation marks, and how this differs throughout English-speaking countries (e.g., "towards" in the UK is often "toward" in the US, and periods and commas always go inside quotation marks in the U.S. but not in Canada).

For examples, see Table 1:

All compound sentences need either a semicolon or a comma conjunction combination. Make sure that a comma is included if there are two independent clauses. Omit the comma if the second clause is subordinate.	Example: Unless the surf is bad, we are going to surf in the morning. Example: The surf is great; we're going surfing.
Commas and periods go inside quotation marks. In the U.S., current style guides place commas and periods inside quotation marks.	Example: She said, "I'm not going with you." Example: While she said, "I'm sick," she still came with us.
Absolutes: Avoid them in most all cases.	Example: Like all other eighteen-year-old girls, I love drama.
Use the subjunctive form of the verb with the words "if" and "wish" (i.e., use "were" not "was").	Example: I wish I were taller. If I were taller, I could play professional volleyball.
Using "so" and "that" right next to each other is often not needed unless you want to make your sentence sound more like an announcement of sorts.	Example: I took a culinary class so ~~that~~ I could show my gratitude toward those who had influenced me.
Using "so" to mean "really" or "very" without using "that" is an error.	Example: I am so grateful to have been a part of a family that has nurtured and emphasized the importance of our heritage. This sentence should read as: I am grateful to have been part of a family **who** has nurtured and emphasized the importance of our heritage."
A person "who" versus a person "that."	Example: I was furious when this happened because the person who was our advisor made the wrong decision.
Only use single quotes when within double quotes. (In UK English, the two would be reversed.)	Example: She declared, "At that moment, that 'Ah-ha' moment, I decided to completely move in."
No "etc." (which is the abbreviation for et cetera) in formal academic writing in most disciplines.	Example: I would lose the ball, fumble passes, and miss shots, etc. It's enough to phrase this sentence as: I would falter in many ways including losing the ball, fumbling passes, and missing shots.
Avoid exclamation points in academic writing unless you want it to sound like you are yelling.	Example: I got ready and made it to the bus on time. The period works just fine here.
Be especially mindful of singular and plural subjects with subject-verb agreement.	Example: The source of the problems were my father's lack of work. This sentence should read as follows: Example: The source [singular] of the problems was [singular] my father's lack of work.

Colons cannot directly follow verbs.	Example:Incorrect: They all harmoniously incorporate elements such as: romance, humor, and, of course, drama.
	Better: They all harmoniously incorporate elements such as romance, humor, and, of course, drama.
	(The "such as" does the trick.)
Do not address the reader directly (i.e., no "you") unless you mean to.	Example:
	Incorrect: If you need to buy books, you should go to the college bookstore.
	Better: Students who need to buy books can go to the college bookstore.
Avoid italics for emphasis and keep them just for foreign words	Incorrect: And one should *never* follow my footsteps. (The word "never" does not need italicizing.)
The correlative conjunction "not only" needs both words "but" and "also." But the "also" could be replaced by a comma at the end of the sentence and an "as well."	Example: I saw how this was not only a significant aspect of my family but also of my culture. Note that no commas are needed within this sentence. Many times people like to add them with this "not only/but (also)" pair unnecessarily.
When explaining the "reason" for something happening, you almost always do not need the word "why."	Example: It just so happens that teenagers and adults see the world differently, hence the reason [why] adults sometimes cannot comprehend teenage struggles the way teens do. Omit the "why" as it's not needed.

Activities

1. Search your draft using the "find" tool for words like "it," "this," "really," "very," "just" or "you." See if you can find ways to eliminate these words to make your language sharper, more precise.
2. Read the sentences of your essay in backward order, starting with the last sentence in the essay, and then the one above it, all the way up to the first sentence in the essay. This is a great way to find fragments or to hear where the language is repetitive or unclear.
3. Make an appointment with a tutor or your instructor. Ask for help doing a close editing of two paragraphs with an eye to learning how to identify typical errors in your work, and then apply your learning to the rest of your essay.

Further Resources

Purdue University's Online Writing Lab (OWL) provides free writing resources and instructional material. Visit *The Purdue* OWL (Purdue U Writing Lab, 2019).

For further information on the steps of the writing process and tips for each of those steps, read "The Writing Process" by Ali Hal (*Daily Writing Tips* website, 2019).

For an editing checklist by Mignon Fogarty (also known as "Grammar Girl"), visit "Grammar Girl's Editing Checklist" (*Quick and Dirty Tips* website, 2019).

CHAPTER 3. ESSAY STRUCTURE

3.1 Introduction

Photo by Håkon Sataøen on Unsplash

A Student's Story

As it was Isabel's first day of college, she was excited but nervous about returning to school after 30 years outside of the classroom raising children and taking care of the normal family needs. Butterflies took up residence in her stomach. She headed to the campus food court to get a coffee so as to see her through the early morning course

She walked across campus, found the correct classroom, and took a seat. Without any bell to signal the start of class, the instructor entered, introduced himself and shared general information about the English 100 course. Then, he passed out the syllabus and other handouts. After discussing the syllabus and expectations, the instructor discussed how one of the handouts was something called a "writing diagnostic."

When the instructor said the word "diagnostic," Isabel repeated it with heart racing a bit because it seemed like such a loaded word. She settled herself and glanced around the classroom. Some students looked relaxed while others began to sink in their seats. Questions floated about in her head: "How does one write a diagnostic? What are the actual components of an essay? How am I going to get started?" Instead of tangling with these questions on her own, she decided to be brave and ask one of these questions out loud. She raised her hand.

The instructor acknowledged her, so Isabel spoke, "Could you please repeat the instructions? I'd like a better understanding."

Her instructor explained, "You will have one hour to read the article and write an effective essay that has an introduction, body, and conclusion. At the end of the term, you will complete the same assignment, and I will compare your writing to evaluate your improvement. Please consider this diagnostic to be a means of assessing how I, as the instructor, am able to help you develop your writing over the course of this semester. Are there any more questions?"

Isabel felt more at ease when she thought about the essay assignment from this perspective. The diagnostic was no longer a means of proving what she did not know about essays; she understood that it was designed to measure her learning over the next 15 weeks. She looked forward to delving into the process of enhancing the skills she already possessed. This was the reason she enrolled in the class—so that she could gain the skills to progress to a managerial position at her job, help her family, and be a role-model for her children and their children.

In college, students are required to write various types of essays and reports. These types of college-based compositions are written for many reasons, and their respective purpose will determine the type of essay that is written. Regardless of the type of essay, there are general qualities that all essays have, and there are guidelines on how to write an essay.

A paragraph is a collection of sentences related to a main point. An essay is a combination of paragraphs that can be divided into three major sections: an introduction, body paragraphs, and a conclusion. Thus, paragraphs function in a variety of ways.

This chapter provides guidelines for how to structure college-level compositions, but these guidelines are meant to be used as a starting point for essay and report writing. There are various ways of writing at any level of one's education or within the professional world. Formats for essays and reports in college change depending on the course, the instructor, and the overriding goals of the assignment. Thus, writers are encouraged to expand the structure, to be creative, and to find their own writing styles.

3.2 Opening Paragraphs

An introduction exists as the first paragraph in a 5-page essay, and it serves the following purposes:

- Establishes reader interest.
- Introduces the general topic of the essay while establishing the writer's voice, tone, or attitude, toward the subject.
- States the thesis that will be supported in the body paragraphs.

Establishing Reader Interest

Introductions should begin with an engaging lead or opener (sometimes called a "hook" in middle school or high school) that is devised to evoke readers' interest. Capturing readers' attention motivates them to continue reading. Writers can garner a reader's interest by doing the following:

- Beginning by quoting an expert on the respective topic or an inspirational individual.
- Beginning by offering some statistical evidence that is both informative and intriguing.
- Opening with a striking mental image.
- Appealing to the reader's emotions.
- Raising a question or series of questions.
- Presenting an explanation or rationalization for the essay.
- Including a personal anecdote.
- Stating in the middle of a story with the conclusion of the story existing as the first sentence in the conclusion paragraph.

Transition Sentences

After the opener or hook, writers need to add transition sentences that should introduce the readers to the topic by stating general facts or ideas about the subject. These important sentences help readers move or "transition" from the hook toward the thesis statement.

A Strong Thesis Statement

An introduction usually contains a thesis statement (i.e., the main point of the essay). A thesis statement is a promise to the reader about what the essay will be about. A thesis is not the topic itself, but rather the writer's angle on the topic. For whatever topic a professor gives, writers must ask themselves, "What do I want to say about it?" Asking and then answering this question is vital to forming a thesis that is precise, forceful, and confident.

A thesis is usually one sentence long and appears toward the end of the introduction. It is specific, and focuses on one to three points of a single idea—points that are able to be demonstrated in the body. It forecasts the content of the essay and suggests how the writer will organize the information.

Specificity

A thesis statement must concentrate on a specific area of a general topic. The creation of a thesis statement begins when writers choose a broad subject and then narrow it down until they have pinpointed a specific aspect of that topic. For example, healthcare is a broad topic, but a proper thesis statement would focus on a specific area of that topic and essentially answer the following question. "What are the options for individuals without healthcare coverage?"

Precision

A strong thesis statement must be precise enough to allow for a coherent argument and to remain focused on the topic. If the specific topic pertains to options for individuals without healthcare coverage, then the precise thesis statement must make an exact, related, claim, such as the following: "Limited options exist for those who are uninsured by their employers." To elaborate on this topic further, the writer might discuss how limited options impact the lives of the uninsured.

Ability to be Argued

A thesis statement must present a relevant and specific argument. A factual statement is often not considered arguable. A thesis statement contains a point of view that can be supported with evidence.

However, a wise way to think about a thesis statement within a persuasive or "argumentative" essay is to write one that strikes up or furthers a conversation versus creating an argument. Imagine someone reading only your thesis statement and the two of you, then, having a conversation in which you share your stance, your reader shares his or her stance, and you continue your discussion with the information from your body paragraphs.

Ability to be Demonstrated

For any claim in the thesis, the writer must be able to provide reasons and examples for this opinion. Personal observations can help, or the writer can consult outside sources to demonstrate validity. A worthy argument is backed by examples and details.

The demonstration of validity comes from incorporating the voices of the experts—those who have already had their work on your topic published, vetted, and added to the respective canon. Use the strategies of quoting, summarizing, or paraphrasing.

Remember that the only way to hit a word or page requirement when writers feel like they have already said everything is to add examples.

Forcefulness

A thesis statement that is forceful shows readers that the writer is, in fact, making an argument. The tone is assertive and takes a stance that others might oppose.

That being said, college-level thesis statements would do well to not include the word "should," as a means of trying to sound authoritative so as to make a solid argument.

Confidence

In addition to using forcefulness in their thesis statement, writers must also be confident in their claims. Phrases such as "I feel" or "I believe" actually weaken the readers' sense of confidence in what they are reading because these phrases imply that the writer may be the only person who feels this way.

Taking an authoritative stance on the matter persuades readers to have faith in the argument and to open their minds to the point of view of the writer. So, no thesis should contain phrases such as "in my opinion" or "I believe." These statements reduce credibility and weaken the argument.

Each of the following thesis statements meets several of the requirements: specificity, precision, ability to be argued, ability to be demonstrated, forcefulness, and confidence.

- The societal and personal struggles of Troy Maxon in the 1986 play *Fences* symbolize the challenges faced by black men who lived through segregation and integration in the United States, and their life stories can be considered as critical to understand the challenge black men continue to face over thirty years later.
- Closing all American borders for a period of five years is one idea proposed so as to deal with illegal immigration; however, contemporary strategies regarding this issue do not address the essential human right for safety along with the essentials of food, clothing, and shelter.
- J. D. Salinger's character in *Catcher in the Rye*, Holden Caulfield, is a confused and somewhat rebellious young person who voices his disgust with "phonies." Yet, in an effort to protect himself, he acts like a phony on many occasions making him a complicated character within one of Salinger's most celebrated novels.
- Compared to an absolute divorce, a no-fault divorce is less expensive, promotes fairer settlements, and reflects a more realistic view of the causes for marital breakdown, although no divorce is easy since the issues involved extend well beyond the monetary and are usually based in an unfortunate undercurrent of misunderstandings and sorrow.
- Discussing the dangers of illegal drug use is with elementary and middle school students is one method that schools use to help dissuade young people from abusing drugs as they grow up. However, children learn a great deal from what they observe making it imperative that parents monitor what their children watch on tv, see in movies, and glean from their friends and family members.
- In today's challenging professional world, a high school diploma is not a significant enough confirmation of one's education so as to obtain a stable, lucrative, lifelong job. Therefore, many colleges and universities are offering more online courses making it possible for more individuals to work toward a college degree while still working to make a living.

Avoid Weak Thesis Statements

Here are some pitfalls to avoid when composing a thesis:

- A thesis is weak when it is simply a declaration of a subject or a description of what the writer will discuss in the essay. *Weak thesis statement*: My paper will explain why imagination is more important than knowledge. Remember, do not refer to your essay in your essay. By the time one enters college, such strategies for writing thesis statements have passed.
- A thesis is weak when it makes an unreasonable or outrageous claim or insults the opposing side. *Weak thesis statement*: Religious radicals across America are trying to legislate their Puritanical beliefs by banning required high school books.
- A thesis is weak when it contains an obvious fact or something that no one can disagree with or provides a dead end. *Weak thesis statement*: Advertising companies often use sexual or romantic appeal to sell their products.
- A thesis is weak when the statement is too broad. *Weak thesis statement*: The life and presidency of Abraham Lincoln was challenging.

Sources

This section is adapted from OER material from "Writing Introductory and Concluding Paragraphs" and "Developing a Strong, Clear Thesis Statement" in Writing for Success v. 1.0 (2012). Writing for Success was adapted by Saylor Academy under a Creative Commons Attribution-NonCommercial-ShareAlike 3.0 License without attribution as requested by the work's original creator or licensor.

3.3 Body Paragraphs

If the thesis is the roadmap for the essay, then body paragraphs should closely follow that map. The reader should be able to predict what follows an introductory paragraph by simply reading the thesis statement. The body paragraphs present the evidence the reader has gathered to support the overall thesis. Before writers begin to support the thesis within the body paragraphs, they should find information from a variety of sources that support the topic.

Select Primary Support for the Thesis

Without primary support, the argument is not likely to be convincing. Primary support can be described as the major points writers choose to expand on the thesis. It is the most important information they select to argue their chosen points of view. Each point they choose will be incorporated into the topic sentence for each body paragraph they write. The primary foundational points are further supported by evidentiary details within the paragraphs.

Identify the Characteristics of Good Primary Support

In order to fulfill the requirements of good primary support, the information writers choose must meet the following standards:

Be Specific

The main points they make about the thesis and the examples they use to expand on those points need to be specific. Writers use specific examples to provide the evidence and to build upon the general ideas. These types of examples give the reader something narrow to focus on, and, if used properly, they leave little doubt about their claim. General examples, while they convey the necessary information, are not nearly as compelling or useful in writing because they are too obvious and typical.

Be Relevant to the Thesis

Primary support is considered strong when it relates directly to the thesis. Primary support should show, explain, or prove their main argument without delving into irrelevant details. When faced with a great deal of information that could be used to prove the thesis, writers may think all the information should be included in the body paragraphs. However, effective writers resist the temptation to lose focus. Good writers choose examples wisely by making sure they directly connect to the thesis.

Add Details

The thesis, while specific, should not be very detailed. Discussion develops in the body paragraphs. Using detailed support shows readers that the writer has considered all the facts and chosen only the most precise details to enhance the point of view.

Prewrite to Identify Primary Supporting Points for a Thesis Statement

When writers brainstorm on a topic, they essentially make a list of examples or reasons they support the stance. Stemming from each point, the writer should provide details to support those reasons. After prewriting, the writer is then able to look back at the information and choose the most compelling pieces to use in writing body paragraphs.

Select the Most Effective Primary Supporting Points for a Thesis Statement

After writers have engaged in prewriting to formulate working thesis statements, they may have generated a large amount of information, which may be edited later. It is helpful to remember that primary support must be relevant to the thesis. Focusing on the main argument, any ideas that do not directly relate to it can be deleted. Omitting unrelated ideas ensures that writers will use only the most convincing information in their body paragraphs. For many first-year writing assignments, students would do well to choose at least three of the most compelling points. These will serve as the content for the topic sentences that will usually begin each of the body paragraphs.

Body Paragraph Structure

One wat to think about a body paragraph is that it, essentially, consists of three main parts: the main point or topic sentence, information and evidence that supports the main point, and an example of how the information gives foundation to the main point and the essay's overall thesis. The three parts of a paragraph can be referred to as the following:

P = Point

I = Information

E = Explanation

An Example of Abbreviated Version of P.I.E.

As a pedestrian in Hawai'i, it is important to be aware of one's surroundings. In 2018, 43 pedestrians died in car accidents (Gordon 3). Hawai'i's roadways can be dangerous, and being vigilant is necessary in order to increase pedestrian safety.

Point: As a pedestrian in Hawai'i, it is important to be aware of your surroundings.

Information: In 2018, 43 pedestrians died in car accident.

Explanation: Hawai'i's roadways can be dangerous, and being vigilant is necessary to increase pedestrian safety.

Use Transitions

Transitional words and phrases help to organize an essay and improve clarity for the reader. Some examples of transitions can be found at "Transitional Devices," The Purdue Purdue Online Writing Lab (OWL).

Activities

1. Write a paragraph that contains a main point, follow-up and substantial information, and an explanation about how that information relates to the main point of the paragraph or to the overall thesis of the essay. The topic of your paragraph is up to you. What topic would you like to write about?

   P: What is the main point of your paragraph?

   I: What information backs up your point?

   E: Explain how this information proves that your main point is correct.

   Combine these three parts to form a paragraph.

Further Resources

Ashford University Writing Center: "Essay Development: Good paragraph development: as easy as P.I.E." *Writing resources*.

Works Cited

"43 pedestrians died on Hawaii roadways in 2018. That's more than the number killed in vehicles." *HawaiiNewsNow*, 3 January 2019.

Sources

Parts of this section are adapted from OER material from "Writing Body Paragraphs" in *Writing for Success* v. 1.0 (2012). Writing for Success was adapted by Saylor Academy under a Creative Commons Attribution-NonCommercial-ShareAlike 3.0 License without attribution as requested by the work's original creator or licensor.

3.4 Conclusions

Writing a Conclusion

It is not unusual to want to rush when approaching the conclusion, and even experienced writers may fade during the labor of writing an essay. However, what good writers remember is that it is vital to put just as much attention into the conclusion as in the rest of the essay. After all, a hasty ending can undermine an otherwise strong essay.

A conclusion that does not correspond with the rest of the essay, has loose ends, or is unorganized can unsettle the reader and raise doubts about the entire essay. However, if the student has worked hard to write the introduction and body, the conclusion can often be the most logical part to compose.

The Anatomy of a Strong Conclusion

The ideas in the conclusion must conform to the rest of the essay. But in a sense it's easier to think of the conclusion of an essay as making the essay come full circle.

When students are asked what they think about writing conclusions to essays, the response is usually less than enthusiastic. When asked what makes conclusion paragraphs an unsatisfying part of their essay, the responses are often the same.

"I have nothing else to say. I've already said everything."

"I know I'm supposed to summarize my main points, but I feel stupid doing that when I just stated all those points."

A conclusion paragraph that is based primarily in summary is also less than satisfying for readers. It feels almost disrespectful in that a reader might think, "I just read all of that. Do you think I already forgot your main points?"

The good thing is that there's a model that exists for writing conclusion paragraphs for standard essays that lets students forget the summary and leave readers nodding in agreement. The easiest way to craft this style of conclusion paragraph is to model it after the introduction.

A typical introduction, even at the freshman level in college, is formatted as follows:

1. Start with a hook (often called an "opener" or a "lead" in college).
2. Create a few transition sentences that move the reader along from opener to thesis statement.
3. State the thesis.

Then, once all the body paragraphs have been carefully crafted, students are ready to write the conclusion. But, again, everything has been said. So the trick is not to even think about "the conclusion." Instead, they should scroll up to the very beginning of their essay and remind themselves about how it all started. The following exists as an innovative way to write a great conclusion paragraph.

1. Revisit the hook. (If the writer started with a quote, offer another quote. If the writer started with statistics, offer more statistics. If the writer asked a question, answer the question. The reader will get a sense of hearing something like that before and will anticipate that the end of the essay is on its way.)

2. Restate the thesis. (Restating the thesis is important because it reminds the reader of the major arguments the writer has been trying to prove. Sometimes instructors suggest restating the thesis at the beginning of the conclusion, but then students are setting themselves up to have nothing left to say but to summarize.)

3. Finish with a twist. (This final commentary often does particularly well when a sort of global extension is made. If the student's essay is about current strategies being used to combat the devastation associated with the Pacific trash vortex, then a final statement could be something like the following: "Clearly the devastation related to the Pacific trash vortex is far-reaching and has effects beyond sea life and coastal societies. More significant, though, is the fact that human beings live every day as a more globalized society in which we have more in common than many continue to think. Since the Pacific Ocean is the largest and deepest ocean on the planet, it is even more important that we, collectively, give it our greatest care.")

Students also like to finish with a final emphatic statement. This strong closing statement will cause their readers to continue thinking about the implications of their essay; it will make their conclusion, and thus their essay, more memorable. Another powerful technique is to challenge their readers to make changes in either their thoughts or their actions. Challenging their readers to see the subject through new eyes is a powerful way to ease the readers out of the essay.

When closing the essay, writers should not express that they are drawing to a close. Statements such as "In conclusion," "It is clear that," "As you can see," or "In summation" are unnecessary and can be considered trite.

It is wise to avoid doing any of the following in a conclusion:

- Introducing new material
- Contradicting the thesis
- Changing the thesis
- Using apologies or disclaimers

Introducing new material in conclusions has an unsettling effect on readers. Raising new points makes reader want more information, which the writer could not possibly provide in the limited space of the final paragraph.

Contradicting or changing the thesis statement causes readers to think that they do not actually have conviction about the topic. After all, they have spent several paragraphs adhering to a singular point of view. When they change sides or open up their point of view in the conclusion, the reader becomes less inclined to believe the original argument.

By apologizing for the opinion or stating what is tough to digest, the writer is in fact admitting that even they know what they have discussed is irrelevant or unconvincing. They do not want readers to feel this way. Effective writers stand by their thesis statement and do not stray from it.

Sources

This section is adapted from OER material from "Writing Introductory and Concluding Paragraphs" in *Writing for Success* v. 1.0 (2012). Writing for Success was adapted by Saylor Academy under a Creative

Commons Attribution-NonCommercial-ShareAlike 3.0 License without attribution as requested by the work's original creator or licensor.

CHAPTER 4. TYPES OF ESSAYS

4.1 Introduction

Photo by Helloquence on Unsplash

Learning Objectives

Student will be able to do the following after reading this chapter:

- Apply essay structure to various rhetorical modes.
- Provide the required components of a specific essay assignment.

A Student's Story

David asked his instructor why students were required to write different types of essays. Instructor Kahaiali'i explained that learning to do a variety of types of writing allows students to determine the best way to approach a range of writing situations in the future.

"In life, an essay you might write to the newspaper arguing against building a light rail system in Honolulu might be argumentative, while a report written for a boss that is meant to inform her about a problem in a factory would use an entirely different tone and structure. The ability to be flexible about one's mode, based on circumstances, is useful in the real world.

"For this class, we will learn how to write a variety of types of essays by using mode guidelines. These guidelines provide a clearer idea of expectations for each essay, but you will also learn to be flexible and to experience many types of writing so that you can apply a range of skills to future writing you'll need to do. While we explore four modes of writing in this class, you will discover that the toolkit of writing skills you'll build will allow you to use many modes, as needed, in the future."

David nodded. Although he appreciated that this course was going to be challenging, he knew that he was improving his skills for the job market. Since written communication skills are in demand, he realized the importance of learning these skills.

The Rhetorical Modes

Rhetorical modes, also known as patterns of development or genres, are simply the ways in which people effectively communicate through language. Sometimes writers incorporate a variety of modes in any one essay. For example, a persuasive essay may include paragraphs showing cause and effect, description, and narrative. The rhetorical mode writers choose depends on the purpose for writing. Rhetorical modes are a set of tools that will allow students greater flexibility and effectiveness in communicating with their audience and expressing ideas.

Here are typical modes of essays taught in first-year writing courses:

- **Cause and effect** discusses the relationship between causes and effects, starting either with causes or effects, and using facts to explain how they are linked.
- **Classification and division**, often used in science, takes large ideas and divides them into manageable chunks of information, classifying and organizing them into types and parts.
- **Comparison and contrast** analyzes the similarities and/or differences between two subjects to learn or discuss them more deeply.
- **Definition** clarifies the meaning of terms and concepts, providing context and description for deeper understanding of those ideas.
- **Description** provides detailed information using adjectives that appeal to the five senses (what people see, hear, smell, taste, and touch) as well as other vivid details that help readers visualize or understand an item or concept.
- **Evaluation** analyzes and judges the value and merit of an essay, a concept, or topic.
- **Illustration** provides examples and evidence in detail to support, explain, and analyze a main point or idea.
- **Narrative** uses fictional or nonfictional stories in a chronological sequence of events, often including detailed descriptions and appeals to the senses and emotions of readers while storytelling to reveal a theme or moment.
- **Persuasion** (i.e., argumentation) logically attempts to convince readers to agree with an opinion or take an action; the argument also acknowledges opposing viewpoints and accommodates and/or refutes them with diplomatic

and respectful language, as well as provides precise and accurate evidence and other expert supporting details.

- **Process analysis** describes and explains, step by step, chronologically, in detail, and with precision and accuracy, how to do something or how something works.

This chapter will focus on the narrative, evaluative, process analysis, and persuasive rhetorical modes.

An introduction to college writing is based on the understanding that the primary underlying skills needed for academic writing involve summary, analysis, and synthesis of information into one's own words, citing sources as needed, and analyzing and evaluating ideas with the confidence of one who feels part of a given community. The skills needed for good writing do not just consist of memorizing rules. Instead, they come from a skills-based approach through reading analytically the work of others and discussing and writing to learn concepts thoroughly and deeply. The writing skills come from mirroring the writing elements that suit each individual student with support from well-researched material. Then students show their growth by embracing these skills in writing.

Each of the following sections provides links to real student essays to help students conceptualize and produce essays in various modes. These samples should be used as guidelines to help meet essay expectations, and should not be substituted for students' original ideas.

Activities

1. Read a printed or online essay or article. A letter to the editor or an editorial from a newspaper would be perfect. Then, with a partner, identify the modes of writing found in the essay. Analyze the different choices the writer has made about language and organization to express a point of view.
2. Select, read, and annotate a sample student essay in a specific style as provided in this link. Note in the margins or on another sheet of paper what rhetorical mode each paragraph uses, how those modes and paragraphs support the overall rhetorical mode of the essay, and whether each paragraph does so successfully or not. Discuss in teams of four and summarize findings to report to the rest of the class.

Sources

4.2 Narration

The Purpose of Narrative Writing

The purpose of narrative writing is to tell stories. Any time a person tells a story to a friend or family member about an event or incident, the individual engages in a form of narration. A narrative can be factual or fictional. A factual story is one that is based on actual events as they unfolded in real life. A fictional story is made up, or imagined; the writer of a fictional story can create characters and events as desired.

The big distinction between factual and fictional narratives is based on the writer's purpose. The writers of factual stories try to recount events as they actually happened, but writers of fictional stories can depart from real people and events because the writers' intentions are not to describe real-life events. Biographies and memoirs are examples of factual stories, whereas novels and short stories are examples of fictional stories.

Because the line between fact and fiction can often blur, it is helpful for writers to understand their purpose from the beginning. Is it important that writers recount history, either their own or someone else's? Or does their interest lie in reshaping the world in their own image—depending on how writers would like to see it or how they imagine it could be? Our answers will go a long way in shaping the stories people tell.

Ultimately, whether the story is fact or fiction, narrative writing tries to relay a series of events in an emotionally engaging way. Authors want the audience to be moved by their stories—through laughter, sympathy, fear, anger, and so on. The more clearly they tell their stories, the more emotionally engaged the audience is likely to be.

The Structure of a Narrative Essay

Major narrative events are most often conveyed in chronological order—the order in which events unfold from first to last. Stories typically have a beginning, a middle, and an end, and events are typically organized by time. Certain transitional words and phrases aid in keeping the reader oriented in the sequencing of a story.

The following are the other basic components of a narrative:

- Plot. The events as they unfold in sequence.
- Characters. The people who inhabit the story and move it forward. Typically, there are minor characters and main characters. The minor characters generally play supporting roles to the main character, or the protagonist.
- Conflict. The primary problem or obstacle that unfolds in the plot that the protagonist must solve or overcome by the end of the narrative. The way in which the protagonist resolves the conflict of the plot results in the theme of the narrative.
- Theme. The ultimate message the narrative is trying to express can be either explicit or implicit.

Writing a Narrative Essay

When writing a narrative essay, authors begin by deciding whether to write a factual or fictional story. Next, they engage in prewriting strategies such as freewriting about topics that are of general interest to them.

Once authors have a general idea of their writing, they sketch out the major events of the story in order to develop the plot. Typically, these events will be revealed chronologically, and will climax at a central conflict that must be resolved by the end of the story. The use of strong details is crucial as authors describe the events and characters in their narrative. They want the readers to emotionally engage with the world that they create.

As always, it is important to start with a strong introduction to hook the reader into wanting to read more. The writer should try opening the essay with an event that is interesting, to introduce the story and get it going. Finally, the conclusion should help resolve the central conflict of the story and impress upon readers the ultimate thesis of the piece. The ending of the story for the main character may be positive or negative. Writers include vivid details in their stories using the five senses so the reader will be able to experience the story.

Code-Switching

Writers use language in a variety of ways. They may use dialogue to convey details that accurately represent the characters and setting of their local story. Or, they may remember the voices of family members. How are they different from other voices? In Hawai'i, there are many languages, including Hawai'i Creole English (Pidgin). Pidgin varies depending on place and time. The spelling of Pidgin words is up to the writer, and it's based on how the words sound. "What" could be spelled "wat" or "wot." Writers may switch between languages (e.g., Pidgin and English) depending on circumstances. This is called code-switching. Accurate representation of dialogue increases the authenticity of a story.

Activities

Most stories have a main character who wants to achieve a goal (e.g., surviving a wipe out while surfing, winning a championship, passing a course, graduating high school). There are obstacles that a main character encounters while trying to achieve a goal (e.g., strong waves, a highly skilled opponent, procrastination, self-doubt). Then the story shows the main character's response to obstacles and whether or not the goal is achieved. If your topic is autobiographical, think of a memory that you don't mind sharing with the class. Regardless if the story is autobiographical or fictional, plan the characters and plot. As you write your short story, the story may turn out differently than you expected, and that's fine. This is a starting point.

I. Character Exercise for Your Narrative Essay

A. How many characters will you have in your story?

B. Who are these characters? Describe each of the characters. For each character, list information on their backstory, their qualities, their goals/desires. How will these characters interact with one another?

C. Will you use first person ("I") or third person ("He/She") to tell this story?

D. Whose point of view will you tell the story from? Through which character's eyes will the reader experience the story from?

II. Plot Exercise for Your Narrative

    A. Introduction and Rising Action

    1. Who is the main character (protagonist) of this story?

    2. What is the main character's goal/desire?

    3. Who/what is the obstacle your main character experiences when trying to achieve a goal/desire?

    4. What does the main character do when encountering this obstacle?

    B. Climax

    1. Is the main character successful or unsuccessful in achieving his/her goal/desire?

    C. Falling Action

    1. What happens after the climax?

    D. Resolution

    1. What happens at the end of the story? Is this a happy ending? What is the lesson learned?

    E. Setting

    1. Where does the story take place?

Sources

Parts of this section is adapted from OER material from "Narration" in *Writing for Success* v. 1.0 (2012). Writing for Success was adapted by Saylor Academy under a Creative Commons Attribution-NonCommercial-ShareAlike 3.0 License without attribution as requested by the work's original creator or licensor.

The section on Code-Switching and other parts is original work by the authors of this text.

4.3 Process Analysis

The Purpose of a Process Analysis

A process analysis essay explains how to do something or how something works. In either case, the formula for a process analysis essay remains the same. The process is articulated into clear, definitive steps. Almost everything writers do involves following a step-by-step process. From riding a bike as children to learning various jobs as adults, writers initially needed instructions to effectively execute the task. Likewise, they have likely had to instruct others, so they know how important good directions are—and how frustrating it is when they are poorly written.

The Structure of a Process Analysis

The process analysis essay opens with a discussion of the process and a thesis statement that states the goal of the process. The organization of a process analysis essay typically follows chronological order. The steps of the process are conveyed in the order in which they usually occur.

Body paragraphs will be constructed based on the aforementioned steps. If a particular step is complicated and needs a lot of explaining, then it will likely take up a paragraph on its own. But if a series of simple steps is easier to understand, then the steps can be grouped into a single paragraph. Words such as first, second, third, next, and finally, are helpful cues to orient the reader and organize the content of essay.

Writing a Process Analysis Essay

1. Choose a topic that is interesting, is relatively complex, and can be explained in a series of steps.
2. As with other rhetorical writing modes, choose a process that you know well so you can more easily describe the finer details of each step in the process. A thesis statement should come at the end of an introduction, and it should state the final outcome of the process one is describing.
3. Body paragraphs are composed of the steps in the process. Each step should be expressed using strong details and clear examples. Use time transition phrases to help organize steps in the process and to orient the reader.
4. The conclusion should thoroughly describe the result of the process described in the body paragraphs.

Activities

1. In the writing process, it's important to brainstorm and organize your thoughts. Write a list of ten

processes that you are familiar with (e.g., cooking rice, surfing, playing a game). Be daring. Include processes that others may not be familiar with. From this list, circle three processes that you are comfortable explaining. Pick one process. What process did you pick?

2. Create an outline or list that includes instructions that a person needs to do to complete this process. Imagine a person who has never done this process before. Show your outline or list to a person in class. Based on this information, is there a clear picture of how to complete this task? Is the person able to perform this task? What instructions need to be added, changed, or deleted? As an additional step, the person could follow instructions to actually perform this task.

Further Resources

See examples of students' essays in *Mānoa Horizons: A Journal of Undergraduate Research, Creative Work, and Innovation* (University of Hawaiʻi at Mānoa, 2019).

Sources

4.4 Evaluation

This section discusses the purpose and structure of evaluation, as many students prepare to write their own evaluative essays.

The Purpose of Evaluative Writing

Writers evaluate arguments in order to present an informed and well-reasoned judgment about a subject. While the evaluation will be based on their opinion, it should not seem opinionated. Instead, it should aim to be reasonable and unbiased. This is achieved through developing a solid judgment, selecting appropriate criteria to evaluate the subject, and providing clear evidence to support the criteria.

Evaluation is a type of writing that has many real-world applications. Anything can be evaluated. For example, evaluations of movies, restaurants, books, and technology ourselves are all real-world evaluations.

The Structure of an Evaluation Essay

Evaluation essays are structured as follows.

Subject

First, the essay will present the **subject**. What is being evaluated? Why? The essay begins with the writer giving any details needed about the subject.

Judgement

Next, the essay needs to provide a **judgment** about a subject. This is the thesis of the essay, and it states whether the subject is good or bad based on how it meets the stated criteria.

Criteria

The body of the essay will contain the **criteria** used to evaluate the subject. In an evaluation essay, the criteria must be appropriate for evaluating the subject under consideration. Appropriate criteria will help to keep the essay from seeming biased or unreasonable. If authors evaluated the quality of a movie based on the snacks sold at the snack bar, that would make them seem unreasonable, and their evaluation may be disregarded because of it.

Evidence

The **evidence** of an evaluation essay consists of the supporting details authors provide based on their judgment of the criteria.

For example, if the subject of an evaluation is a restaurant, a judgment could be "Kay's Bistro provides an unrivaled experience in fine dining." Some authors evaluate fine dining restaurants by identifying appropriate criteria in order to rate the establishment's food quality, service, and atmosphere. The examples are the evidence.

Another example of evaluation is literary analysis; judgments may be made about a character in the story based on the character's actions, characteristics, and past history within the story. The scenes in the story are evidence for why readers have a certain opinion of the character.

Job applications and interviews are more examples of evaluations. Based on certain criteria, management and hiring committees determine which applicants will be considered for an interview and which applicant will be hired.

Activities

1. Evaluate a restaurant. What do you expect in a good restaurant? What criteria determines whether a restaurant is good?
2. List three criteria that you will use to evaluate a restaurant. Then dine there. Afterwards, explain whether or not the restaurant meets each criteria, and include evidence (qualities from the restaurant) that backs your evaluation.
3. Give the restaurant a star rating. (5 Stars: Excellent, 4 Stars: Very Good, 3 Stars: Good, 2 Stars: Fair, 1 Star: Poor). Explain why the restaurant earned this star rating.

Further Resources

See examples of students' essays in Mānoa Horizons: A Journal of Undergraduate Research, Creative Work, and Innovation (University of Hawai'i at Mānoa, 2019).

Sources

Parts of this section are adapted from OER material from Susan Wood, "Evaluation Essay," *Leeward* CC ENG 100 OER, licensed under the Creative Commons Attribution-NonCommercial-ShareAlike 4.0 International License. Original content contributed by Susan Wood.

4.5 Persuasion

Writers of persuasive essays take a stand on a controversial issue and give well-researched arguments to support this position. This section will help students define the persuasive essay as well as understand its purpose and structure.

What is an Argument?

In today's society, arguments are all around us, in our every waking moment throughout the day, whether in online ads or in the messages one reads on one's favorite box of cereal. The ability to think critically in terms of deciding what to believe is highly important due to the fact that individuals are bombarded by arguments, on the internet and elsewhere, on a daily basis. Deciding what arguments to accept or reject not only makes for a good essay, but has implications for success in life and for one's future career.

Understanding the nature of argument is essential to writing a good persuasive essay. So, what is argument? It is not the act of proving who is right or wrong. Television and social media convey argument as a means of proving one's point for the sake of arguing. This is not argument. Ancient rhetoricians such as Aristotle, Plato, and Socrates understood argument in terms of truth-seeking, and conceptualized it as a means of preventing war. In this vein, good writers engage in truth-seeking to find out what is valid so that they may communicate truths to others. Sometimes in this process of truth-seeking, the writers themselves may change their minds on a given topic. Leaders such as Queen Lili'uokalani and Dr Martin Luther King, Jr. demonstrate argument as a means of engaging in truth-seeking. See A Letter of Protest (Queen Lili'uokalani of Hawai'i, 1898) and Letter from a Birmingham Jail (Dr. Martin Luther King, Jr., AU, University of Alabama, April 16, 1963).

Structure of a Persuasive Essay

Before students begin creating persuasive essays, they should engage in preliminary research. Persuasive essays often include quotes or paraphrases from experts or statistics from academic studies. These essays must also demonstrate the writer's ability to think critically and to avoid logical errors.

Note: Persuasive essays often require research, so students should see the Research and Plagiarism chapter of this text before drafting the essay.

After writers have conducted some preliminary research to enter the conversation, they will be ready to begin writing. Drafting should include at least four aspects:

- Introduction and thesis
- Strong arguments and evidence in support of thesis
- Opposing and qualifying ideas
- A compelling and satisfying conclusion

Creating an Introduction and Thesis

The persuasive essay begins with an engaging introduction that presents the general issue. The role of this paragraph is to do the following:

- Create interest.
- Introduce a controversial topic.
- Include a thesis statement that clearly presents the writer's position on the chosen issue, and the major points to be discussed. Instructors will give students further guidelines on where the thesis should appear, but it is usually located at the very end of the introduction.

Strong Arguments and Evidence in Support of the Thesis

The body of the persuasive essay presents the reasons for the writer's position on the issue. Writers should provide at least three solid reasons for their position.

When developing arguments and evidence, a writer would be wise to do the following:

- Provide at least one paragraph for each reason that is presented (though some reasons may require more than one paragraph). Clearly state each reason in a topic sentence.
- Provide sufficient evidence for each reason. Much of the evidence will come from research, though writers can effectively integrate their own knowledge as evidence.
- Explain ideas thoroughly and carefully, connecting one's sources together smoothly and logically.
- Provide follow-up discussion or explanation for the researched information one has provided.
- Remember that arguments are usually "won" or "lost" on the quantity and quality of the evidence.

Ways to Persuade

There are three primary ways to appeal to the emotion and response of readers: ethos, logos, and pathos.

Ethos

Ethos is the appeal to what is right, fair and trustworthy. For example, if Aaron is arguing for more access to parks in Hawai'i for individuals who are disabled, he could do so by pointing out that many citizens who happen to have some sort of disability pay taxes that support these parks and yet are denied access simply due to design. The unfairness of this situation would appeal to the readers' sense of what is right or fair.

Logos

Logos appeals to the reader's logic and reason. If Aaron is arguing for the need to make college tuition more affordable or even free, such as is the case in Norway, Sweden, and Germany, among other countries, and he uses statistics about the number of students who would not be able to obtain a college degree without some country-wide assistance, he is appealing to his reader's logic.

Pathos

An argument with pathos appeals to the reader's emotions. In his essay in favor of students joining a sports team in high school, he could highlight his own experience of overcoming fears and physical challenges while running in high school. Such an approach would pull the heartstrings of his readers who are touched by his success due to the self-discipline, social connections, and physical strength he developed through running on a team.

Addressing Opposing Ideas and the Author's Position

Any good argument anticipates the opposing arguments and attempts to answer or refute its main points. In refuting the opposing point, writers do the following:

1. Address at least one major opposing point. Writers briefly summarize viewpoints on the other side of the argument.
2. Provide reasons and evidence showing the weaknesses in this opposing idea. They may address more than one opposing viewpoint.

Conclusion: Call to Action

The conclusion should provide insight into the significance of the issue. Most important is the fact that such a conclusion would do well not to use the word "should" as in the following. "In order for the United States to increase college attendance, encourage young people to seek out higher education and advanced knowledge to be used within the professional world, and truly support the process of learning, making college tuition more affordable or even free is key."

If writers have proven their stance within the body paragraphs using examples and quoted, paraphrased, or summarized information from professionals within the given community, a "should" isn't needed because the reader has already been convinced.

Activities

1. Take a look at advertisements for products. How are advertisers trying to persuade you to purchase their product?

    ◦ What facts (logos) does the advertiser provide?
    ◦ What emotions do you feel after viewing the advertisement?
    ◦ What occurred in the advertisement to cause these emotions (pathos)?
    ◦ What occurred in the advertisement that appealed to your sense of morals and ethics (ethos)?
    ◦ Overall, was the advertisement effective to persuade you to purchase their product? Why or why not?

Further Resources

- Read more about writing a thesis statement in the handout by University of North Carolina at Chapel Hill: Thesis Statements, The Writing Center.
- Watch the following video to learn more about persuasive appeals: Ethos, Pathos, Logos
- Read more about counterarguments and the language used to signal the counterargument and refutation in this handout by Harvard College Writing Center: Counterargument, Writing Resources.
- See sample persuasive essays in "Chapter 15: Introduction to Sample Essays," Writing for Success.
- Other sample persuasive essays are "Online Monitoring: A Threat to Employee Privacy in the Wired Workplace"; (Hacker), and "Performance Enhancement through Biotechnology Has No Place in Sports"; (Hacker). These essays are excellent references because they contain notes in the margins that explain the components of the essays and MLA format.
- Purdue Online Writing Lab (OWL). "Transitional Devices," The Purdue OWL.

Works Cited

Hacker, Diana. *Writer's Reference*. Bedford/St. Martins, 2007.

King, Jr., Martin Luther. "Letter from a Birmingham Jail," AU, *University of Alabama*, April 16, 1963.

Lili`uokalani (Queen of Hawai`i). Letter to the U.S. House of Representatives (protesting U.S. assertion of ownership of Hawai`i), U.S. National Archives, Records of the U.S. House of Representatives, Record Group 233, Record HR 55A-H28.3, 19 December 1898.

CHAPTER 5. RESEARCH SKILLS

5.1 Introduction

Photo by Davide Cantelli on Unsplash

Learning Objectives

Students will be able to achieve the following:

- Use all the steps of the research process to write an informed essay or report.
- Generate a suitable area of focus for research-based academic writing.
- Distinguish which sources are credible and appropriate for a college paper.
- Cite quoted, paraphrased, or summarized material in order to appropriately give others credit for their original words, ideas, and overall content.
- Cite resources ethically (without plagiarism).

- Use a style guide to create an academic, properly formatted essay or report.

A Students' Story

Jaden and Karen are two very different students, both of whom are taking English 100. When asked to write a research-based essay, Jaden copies text directly from internet sources and pastes it into his document as he stays up late and tries to meet the morning deadline for turning in his essay. Karen, on the other hand, has been researching for the past four weeks, finding ideal resources, jotting down her own ideas and significant facts into a Google Doc or in her notebook, always recording exactly what page and paragraph number from which the information came. She was able to use the sources she found it a way that is ideal for college-level writing—to allow them to provide support for her own, original, unique ideas.

Karen gave herself time to gain more knowledge and, therefore, more expertise regarding her topic so that all her studying and gained knowledge would help her become informed for this particular research-based assignment, as well as giving her practice for similar writing assignments that would come her way throughout her college career. Karen had based her writing on her own ideas and then cited others' appropriately, which she continued to do throughout the semester. Her professor praised Karen for her creativity, thoroughness, and organization, along with her correctly citing her sources.

As Karen continued to grow in confidence, she decided to apply for a position as a writing tutor through her college's peer mentoring program. Once hired, she would not only earn a paycheck, but she would also gain valuable experience helping others understand the intricacies involved in the research and writing processes while sharing her own stories regarding how to succeed in college.

Jaden, however, was asked by his professor to make an appointment to meet with her. When he arrived at her office, she invited him to take a seat. "Where did you find your content for this report?" she asked.

A bit befuddled, he answered, "Through researching it . . . like with sources I found on the internet and in articles I found about my topic. They're all listed in my Works Cited." He reached for the paper and flipped to the back pages. "See. These sources. And I included the intext citations here." He pointed to another section within the body of his report. "And here."

His professor knew that Jaden's report was not only suffering from his failure to commit to the number of hours necessary for such a research-based project but that he had also never adequately learned how to incorporate the words and ideas of experts of others with his own words and ideas in a way that allowed already-existing information to fortify his original writing . . . not replace it.

Such plagiarism—taking the work of others and using it as his own—could involve department chairs and even college deans, the threat of failing a course, or, in extreme cases, suspension. However, particular consideration needed to be given to the fact that Jaden had been writing his research-based essays like this for years, and he had still made it to college. Was he at fault for beginning his report too late and thinking an all-nighter and what was largely a cut-and-paste job could save him? Certainly. But how many instructors before this had just let it slide because he had "included the intext citations"?

One successful habit Karen used was not only reading but also engaging with the source she discovered during the research process. She interacted with the texts by jotting down observations on printouts of articles regarding what the writers' ideas made her think about. For online sources, she created two columns on a page in her notebook: (1) notes and citations of what the author was saying, and (2) her thoughts, opinions, analysis, or evaluation of each source along with her own, original ideas that came to mind as she was reading.

What Karen did was participate in the existing dialogue about her topic—the conversation that was taking place among the established experts—and contribute by "publishing" (by submitting her essay by the deadline to her professor) her own original ideas as well as her analysis and evaluation of what others said. This practice also resulted in her own synthesis of her previous knowledge with her newly gained knowledge and her continued analytical thinking, innovation, and creation of written knowledge about that topic. She learned that writing allows the individual doing so to enter the conversation, which is what academia, especially at the college level, is all about.

Jaden's instructor helped him understand how to properly incorporate the ideas of others within his essay through using a body paragraph from his own essay that was largely composed from content that he had obtained from an outside source. She asked Jaden to use two different colored highlighters to identify the phrases that were in his own voice and that were written from his own knowledge and those that came from an outside source. The professor explained the 70/30 rule, which says that 70% of an essay should be in the original voice of the writer and a maximum of 30% can be in the voice of an established expert on the subject, noting that some prefer more of a 60/40 percentage.

The instructor showed Jaden how to follow quoted, paraphrased, or summarized content with standard intext citations within parentheses. She also showed him how to intersperse such important information with sentences he crafted on his own. "State it again in your own words. Explain in your own words how that information relates to the overall focus of your section. Connect that information to more information that will follow," she explained. "And when you get to the end of your paragraph with more information from an outside source, finish up with your own wise voice."

"I can do that," Jaden said. "How come nobody ever showed me how to do that? I've been getting away with this kind of research-based writing for years."

The focus of English 100 is the types of writing students will encounter in college and their careers. Most of the majors students choose require them to conduct extensive research all the way through college. So the students' job is to learn how to do it so as to demonstrate their researching skills and increasing knowledge.

An introduction to college writing is based on understanding that the primary underlying skill of academic writing at the college level lies within analysis and the ability to synthesize information into one's own words, citing sources as needed, with the confidence of one who feels part of a given community. The skills needed for good research-based writing involve reading the work of experts, assimilating that information with one's own brilliant (and evolving) ideas, possibly mirroring some of the writing that suits each individual student, and becoming a clear, creative, and confident writer in his or her own right.

5.2 The Research Process

To succeed in college, students need to develop solid research skills that will benefit them throughout and beyond their academic career. They must focus, in and out of class, on doing the following:

- Identifying an area of focus
- Identifying the audience
- Using campus library resources to find information
- Determining if information is scholarly and credible
- Citing sources accurately, avoiding plagiarism, and creating a final written composition using the appropriate style guide

Identifying an Area of Focus

Any student writer's initial task is to make sure he or she understands what the instructor is asking for. Precious time can be wasted if students begin their research without a clear picture of what their end product should look like and how it should read. Once an essay is assigned, and some initial contemplation and research on the student's part, it is a great time to make an appointment with an instructor.

Conscientious college writers begin thinking about and researching essay topics immediately after being given the assignment. As we all know, brainstorming can be a solid way to record important initial ideas. At the end of a brainstorming session, writers can begin to see patterns of interest, which will become perfect places to begin research. Avenues within writer's researching often need to remain fluid initially so student writers can determine what kind of resources are available regarding the respective the topic. This flexibility allows students to narrow or broaden topics into a thesis that might not be obvious at first.

Identifying the Audience

All writing is created for a specific audience. Writers must identify the specific reader they want to reach. If they are writing for a general audience, what is the best way to capture a wide range of readers' interests? Should they provide background information that general readers would not necessarily know? Are they writing for an audience already well versed in this topic, and, if so, does this mean writers can use more scholarly language and include less background information?

Using Campus Library Resources and the Internet to Find Information

Research-based writing is only as credible as the sources the writer uses. Therefore, students should start with the college library catalogs and databases. There, a writer can find reference materials (e.g., encyclopedias and dictionaries), books, multimedia resources, as well as the most valuable resource of all, the college librarian. Librarians are trained with the most up-to-date strategies to access scholarly and popular resources that are available to students and usable for college projects. These days, many of these resources can be accessed online from home, which makes learning to use the tools of the library even more important and valuable.

The internet is increasingly used to find sources for academic essays. However, much of what is found on the web is not appropriate for college work. Note, too, that a simple internet search may not allow students to access full articles of ideal credible and scholarly sources whereas going through one's college or university library main page will allow full and free access.

Some of the skills that good writers use as part of information competency include the following:

- Accessing the library search engines
- Determining the best search terms
- Narrowing or expanding search results
- Finding the best books, articles, and other sources through the library catalog

Determining if Information is Credible

Evaluating the quality of resources is an essential skill, especially in today's world. People are inundated with media of various kinds, much of which tries to get us to buy something or to think in a certain way, so perhaps one of the most essential skills to learn is information literacy. The biggest challenge student researchers have is based in the fact that there is such a vast quantity of information available that could potentially be used for a research-based paper. However, there exists a significant range between highly credible, relevant information and that which is not. Materials found online are usually less reliable than those curated and made available through library resources purchased through the college.

Because "facts" can be accessed in just a few moments, it can be tempting to assume that they are just that—factual. More recently and more often, free online information is not fact, not verifiable through citations, and not credible. In addition, new kinds of sources are available, such as a live news feeds or any one of the array of social media options, thus necessitating a variety of ways of assessing information. As such, understanding how to research is key, especially in this new era when content can be skewed in a number of ways.

Evaluating sources is detective work. The researcher needs to make decisions about what to search for, how to search, and what type of information is credible and academically appropriate. For example, a student who is writing about the Great Pacific Garbage Vortex will find many sources available through library-based searches, as well as through online resources that could be more current. However, information that comes from the website of a company that produces petrochemicals and plastics will not be as valuable as a source that comes from scholarly research found through the UH Library System.

The following are some questions students need to ask of every source they are considering for an academic paper:

- Is this source relevant to the topic? Does it give background, explain concepts, and offer support for or an alternative viewpoint on the topic?
- Is it considered a credible source? What is the expertise of the person who wrote it? How current is it? Where was it published? What was the source of funding for this publication? Would that funding source add bias to the material? Are there references that indicate where the information has come from? Is it scholarly or written for a general audience? What does the language used in the source suggest about the purpose of the piece or the scholarliness of the writers?

Depending on the answers to these questions, writers can feel secure with sources that are relevant and credible. Papers that use high-quality sources get better results and better grades with the sharing of important information with professors and other readers.

Activities

1. Write assignments about a topic that is not only interesting to you, but that also encourages you to write about that topic with a strong sense of responsibility to the larger audience or the greater good. (Readings and assignments are most ideal when they can be individualized, relevant to your major area of academic focus. Suggestions of such essay topics can be found at the end of this chapter.)

2. Researched Persuasive Essay: In two minutes, brainstorm or list the biggest problems you wish could be solved in the world. In another two minutes, list the biggest problems you have noticed in the nation. In one minute, list the biggest problems in your state. In another minute, list the biggest problems in your community, town, area, ahupua'a. Take three minutes to list your personal values, beliefs, and priorities, and number them in order of importance. Then take five minutes to review your prioritized personal lists and select one of the "big problems," from any of the lists, that match up with your values, beliefs, and priorities. This will help you to select topics you care deeply about and can engage with.

3. Once you have selected a topic for a persuasive argument involving research to back up your key idea, spend five minutes freewriting, brainstorming, listing your main claim (i.e., persuasive argument) about a debatable issue. After listing your main claim, list all possible key ideas that back up the main claim, as well as all the solutions and opposing perspectives (i.e., counterclaims) you can think of. Then spend 10 minutes with a partner or a team of three to four peers, discussing your ideas and gathering feedback and additional ideas, and noting down what your partner or team said. Then spend 10 minutes creating an outline or informal list organizing your thesis statement and the key points that become the topic sentences of your paragraphs.

5.3 Citing Sources

Citing Sources Accurately, Avoiding Plagiarism, and Creating a Final Research Project

By using the references page and in-text citations of research articles, Karen was able to scout out even more helpful information on her topic. She learned the value of those in-text citations and lists of works consulted when she was reading something interesting and wanted to learn more. When an article cited the name of the original source's author, title, publication information, and direct online link, she was able to go to the original source and dive deeper into the information she was passionate about learning. She also reviewed her syllabus, the formatting and documentation style it indicated, and the style guides themselves.

Every publisher, profession, and academic discipline has its own style guide, which provides standards, expectations, and guidelines for formatting written work, for documenting research, whether read or conducted, and for citing outside sources that help inform readers and other potential writers. Publishers and professors expect written work (i.e., essays and reports) to meet the standards set in these style guides. Information about the five most important, most common style guides used in academic disciplines can be found in the Further Resources box at the end of this chapter.

A research-based essay that conforms to the conventions of a style guide signals to the reader that the writer has joined the academic conversation and should be taken seriously. It also indicates the writer's respect for the thoughts and ideas of others. In addition, the reader learns where to go to find other information on the topic. When writers do not turn in a research paper with the correct format, it is analogous to showing up in board shorts to a job interview.

Citation Management

While using a style guide requires attention to detail, the process can be simplified by using a variety of free tools that help students make a Works Cited (in MLA) or References (in APA) page. For example, many students use an add-on for Google Docs called EasyBib Bibliography Creator, or Zotero, a free online tool to help students to organize research materials into academic formats.

Another tool is BibMe: Free Bibliography & Citation Maker, and even Purdue OWL offers generator options.

While these tools make many of the tasks of conforming to a style guide easier, students should always check the final outcome with the style guides themselves because the order in which the citation is generated often comes out wrong for various reasons, often because of the way in which the information was entered. It is important for writers to double-check for little "errors" in punctuation and capitalization. Sometimes the generator places titles inaccurately in ALL CAPS. Sometimes hyphens are placed where dashes should be. If the quotation marks and apostrophes are in a serif font in the body of the essay, writers need to be sure the quotation marks and apostrophes look the same in the references section.

Using Sources Correctly

Karen found 15 different sources she could use for her 10-page analytical report for her psychology class. She discovered that only nine were fully credible and appropriate for the topic and for college-level writing. In contrast, Jaden went with the first two sources that popped up in his internet search and copied and pasted paragraphs from the sources directly into his document. In addition, he promptly forgot where he got the information and what the title of each was called. He did not notice if there were author names or publication dates. He did not know what form the list of sources at the end of the paper should be in. All of these oversights lessened the quality of his work. Plagiarism (i.e., using the words and ideas of another writer without proper attribution) could cause Jaden to receive a failing grade for his essay and perhaps be grounds for suspension.

Annotations and Citations: Be Accurate and Precise

Karen consulted various free online guides to ensure that her in-text citations and list of works cited were correct and complete. Jaden had missed this significant information when it had been presented in class. When he had that unfortunate required meeting with his professor regarding his plagiarized essay, the fact that he did not understand the importance of this element in the process of crafting his essay was a glaring concern. Was it one that was fixable within his essay at this point in the semester? Not likely.

Annotation: The Basics

It is important to take notes when researching, and to accurately use credible sources. When deep-diving into the information written by others, be sure to take accurate notes, indicating the following:

- Whether the source material borrowed is verbatim (i.e., copied word for word) or paraphrased and summarized (i.e., rewritten in one's own words)
- The page number and paragraph number, if identifiable, from which the information came
- The publication information required for the citation at the end in the style that the professor requires

For MLA-style papers, information such as the author's first and last name, the title of the article, title of the book, publication, magazine, or webpage, publication volume, number, or series, name of the publisher, publication date, and URL, DOI, or link (if the source is online) are all required.

Note: MLA uses the word "Accessed" to denote the date on which the information on the web was obtained. However, for the newest edition MLA 8, it is not required to add this information at the end of the Works Cited entry, but it is especially encouraged when there is no copyright date listed on a website.

Helpful Annotation Tools

Besides paper, index cards or sticky notes, there are various other methods and software applications (apps) with which to organize source citations, quotations, paraphrases, and summaries, along with one's own ideas and outlines. These include Microsoft Onenote, Evernote, and EndNote.

Documentation and Citation

To use sources correctly and appropriately, give appropriate credit following the sentence, paragraph, or general area that uses outside source information.

For MLA style, use in-text citations following direct quotes, paraphrasing, or summarizing, with author(s) last name(s) and page numbers (if available) within parentheses. (The information in the in-text citation will be whatever the first word is in the Works Cited entry. For that reason, it can be easier to add in in-text citations after the Works Cited page has been created.)

For example, see the following:

"The opioid epidemic has expanded exponentially in the past five years" (McKenna 5).

Or, if using a signal phrase, the in-text citation will be like this:

The opioid epidemic has expanded exponentially in the past five years" (5).

For APA style, writers use the author(s) last name(s) followed by a comma and the year of publication.

"The opioid epidemic has expanded exponentially in the past five years" (McKenna, 2018).

Essentially, all individuals deserve credit for their hard work. But even more important is the fact the student's own ideas, as expressed through writing, are what professors look for. The student's words should be informed by the research, not usurped by it. Since the grade one earns is based on the value of the content and how it is communicated through the written word, it's the student's voice that matters to the professor. So writers should supplement and support the original content by incorporating outside sources through quoting, paraphrasing, summarizing, or paraphrasing, following each instance with in-text citations.

Quote. To repeat or copy a group of words from a document or speech, typically with an indication that one is not the original author or speaker. Quotes work well when the material is difficult to paraphrase in a unique way.

Paraphrase. To express the meaning of something written or spoken using different words, especially to achieve greater clarity.

Summarize. To give a brief statement of the main points of something longer.

An important thing to remember about quoting is that sometimes the material a writer would like to borrow directly is longer than four lines of typed text. If this is the case, writers will need to use something called an "extract," sometimes referred to as a "block quote." In an extract or block quote, the quotation marks are removed from the quoted material, and the entire section being quoted is indented one tab from the left-hand margin. Note that in this case the period goes before the in-text citation.

A Word About "Drive-By" Citations

Another strategy some writers use is what some educators call "drive-by" citations. These are references to a work that make a very quick appearance. Then the student writer moves on without discussing the connection between the student's work and the ideas in the citation. This kind of incorporation of the words or ideas of others is to be avoided as it adds little value.

The List at the End of the Paper

To use sources correctly, it's also critically important to give appropriate credit in a list at the end of any college research paper. There are a variety of names and titles for these lists, depending on the style and style guides.

Works Cited (MLA). A Works Cited list is an alphabetical list of works cited, or sources specifically referenced in the body of the paper. All works that have been quoted or paraphrased should be included. Works read but not referenced in the body of the paper should be left off this list.

References (APA). A References list is similar to a Works Cited list; this is the term used when citing sources using APA (American Psychological Association) style. The page should be titled "References" and arranged alphabetically by author last name.

Bibliography (APA). A Bibliography lists all the material consulted in preparing an essay, whether the essay has actually referred to and cited the work or not.

Annotated Bibliography. An annotated bibliography is a list of citations of books, articles, and documents. Each citation is followed by a brief (usually about 150 words) descriptive and evaluative paragraph–the annotation. The purpose of the annotation is to inform the reader of the relevance, accuracy, and quality of the sources cited.

Notes

Using notes and bibliography is preferred by those writing within the humanities, including literature, history, and the arts. With this approach, sources are cited in numbered footnotes or endnotes. Each note corresponds to a superscript (raised) numeral within the document. Sources are also usually listed in a separate bibliography.

The author-date approach is more common in the sciences and social sciences. With this approach, sources are briefly cited in the document, usually in parentheses, by author last name and year of publication. Each in-text citation matches up with an entry in a Reference list, where full bibliographic information is provided.

Plagiarism, Ethics, and Academic Integrity

When Jaden was being reprimanded by his professor, he did not understand what he had done wrong. He had copied and pasted text before, and his high school teachers had not noticed. Now he could lose the ability to complete his other courses, if he was expelled from college. He could even lose the opportunity to return to the campus for any future pursuits. He requested help, and the Professor and Dean sent him to the College Writing Center for additional tutoring on research methods and academic integrity, and to the Learning Center for mentoring and counseling about time management, prioritization, and focus. As a new writing tutor, Karen helped Jaden to read and annotate the syllabus information on academic integrity, plagiarism, and online resources for research.

Academic honesty is fundamental in a college environment. It is essential for academic writers to understand the ethical use of other people's words and ideas. College instructors expect students to fulfill their academic obligations through honest and independent effort. Students need to demonstrate academic integrity: the respectful and truthful attribution of credit to those who have provided words and ideas that are used in research assignments. The reason that plagiarism is treated seriously at the college is that it is seen as an academic crime or simply cheating.

Tips for Avoiding Plagiarism

Research writing should present a writer's thinking, supported and illuminated by the thinking and writing of others. Distinguishing between the two is paramount to academic integrity. Desperate students sometimes purchase an essay from a website and submit it as original course work. More often, writers plagiarize due to sloppiness, haste or ignorance. To avoid unintentional plagiarism, writers need to do the following:

- Understand what types of information must be cited
- Understand what constitutes fair use of a source
- Keep source materials and notes carefully organized
- Distinguish what information is composed of facts or general statements that are common knowledge

What is Common knowledge? Common knowledge is a fact or general statement that is commonly known. For example, a writer would not need to cite the statement that fruit juices contain sugar; this is well known and well-documented. However, if a writer explained the differences between the chemical structures of the glucose molecule and how sugar is related to today's levels of obesity in America, a citation would be necessary. When in doubt, cite.

What is Fair Use? Writers are allowed to quote, paraphrase, or summarize material from previously published works without formally obtaining the copyright holder's permission. The concept of "fair use" means that writers may legitimately use brief excerpts from source material to support and develop their own ideas. For instance, a journalist might excerpt a few lines from a recently released film when writing a movie review. However, quoting or paraphrasing another's work at excessive length, to the extent that large sections of the writing are unoriginal, is not fair use.

The 70/30 and 15% Rules: The 70/30 Rule says that approximately 70% of the written content should be original words and ideas from the student writer, with up to 30% from outside sources. The 15% Rule is that student writers should never use more than 15% of direct quotes from sources. If the writing goes over this amount, the voice of the student is not strong enough.

Value Your Own Voice

Plagiarism is the result of students who lack confidence in their ability to communicate in writing. It also frequently happens because students have not yet mastered the college success skills of time management, prioritization, and focus. In addition, some students value the ethos and authority of the writing of experts, even at the cost of valuing their own words, phrasing, and ideas. They may be afraid to say things in their own way. But college is partly about students finding their own voices and building confidence in communicating. Students remember that quotes and sources shouldn't drive their papers. Their own original ideas should.

Here are two techniques one could use to avoid plagiarism when researching and writing using sources:

- After reading and annotating a research report, put it aside. Without looking at it, freewrite a summary.
- Only use direct quotes when a source's original words provide a unique and critical perspective that can't be paraphrased or briefly summarized.

A Note About Time Management While Researching

Students make time for research in order to develop important college success skills. When professors introduce writing assignments based on research, they hope that students will be excited about their potential topics. Professors encourage students to start researching as soon as possible, so they see what problems rise to the surface: What sources have already been written about the topic? Who is studying and writing about the same area? What makes that individual, researcher, and expert worth listening to? And what gives their work authority and credibility?

Some college students vastly underestimate the time needed to conduct the kind of research that gives them expertise on a topic. Those with lower grades have often simply not planned, nor have they spent enough time immersing themselves in the research process and content so they can become more knowledgeable or "expert" on the field. This is often when plagiarizing happens. Time management is essential.

Activities

- Put away a plagiarized essay and tell the instructor or peer mentor what you wrote, recalling your ideas in your own words (mentioning a source or two as appropriate). You talk; the instructor or peer mentor types. Then review what was typed and see how powerful and effective your own words were. You should gain increased confidence in your own voice and ability to communicate.
- Take out two highlighters and draw through your own words with one color, and through information from an outside source with another color. Learn to recognize how much of the content is your own, and learn the 70/30 Rule.

Further Resources

For each of these styles, a link to a free online guide from Purdue University's Online Writing Lab (OWL) is provided. Should the links to specific pages change, please search the The Purdue OWL. Purdue Online Writing Lab, 2019.

"MLA (Modern Language Association): The arts and humanities." The Purdue OWL. Purdue Online Writing Lab, 2019.

"American Psychological Association (APA): Education, psychology, and the social sciences." The Purdue OWL. Purdue Online Writing Lab, 2019.

"The Chicago Manual of Style (CMOS): The world of publishing." The Purdue OWL. Purdue Online Writing Lab, 2019.

"Associated Press (AP): Journalism such as magazines and newspapers." The Purdue OWL. Purdue Online Writing Lab, 2019.

"American Medical Association (AMA): Medicine, health, and biological sciences." The Purdue OWL. Purdue Online Writing Lab, 2019.

This is where you can add appendices or other back matter.

Appendix 1. Place-Based and Culture-Based Readings

Photo by Jeremy Bishop on Unsplash

It is important to respect, acknowledge, and include place-based, culture-based, and culturally-relevant readings for courses. Including readings that accurately represent communities that students are familiar with engages and empowers students and enhances their knowledge of rich, culturally diverse literature. Students identify with issues and places relevant to their lives and communities, and students feel that their identities and traditions are important and respected. Many students are interested in literature from multiple cultures and places, including Hawai'i.

Hawai'i is the most diverse state in the United States. In Hawai'i's past, people from many nations immigrated to work on the plantations. To communicate with each other, people speaking multiple languages used words from English and Hawaiian (the standard and official languages of Hawai'i), as well as various immigrant languages, creating Pidgin, which evolved into Hawai'i Creole English (still known as Pidgin today). Pidgin is now a language acknowledged by the U.S. Census. It is common for Hawai'i residents to code-switch between English and Pidgin, as it is for people in other nations to code-switch between their language and English.

Included are some online resources for place-based and culture-based readings and videos. There are many place-based and culture-based sources. Listed below are a few examples. Students are encouraged to seek more sources, and many faculty, librarians, and staff are eager to contribute more place-based and culture-based sources.

Appendix 2. Online Videos and Readings

Videos

For a series of author interviews and literary readings recorded on the Leeward Community College campus, visit The Reading Room, EMC Leeward CC.

Leeward Community College hosts a collection of instructional videos on their Youtube Channel, EMC Leeward CC.

Website

Pūpū A ʻO ʻEwa is a Leeward Community College online project publishing Native Hawaiian writing and art.

Journals

Mānoa Horizons is an annual journal of peer-reviewed, undergraduate-student research, creative work, and innovation at the University of Hawaiʻi at Mānoa.

For a collection of linked poetry, visit the Renshi Series by *Bamboo Ridge: A Journal of Hawaiʻi Literature and Arts*.

The Hawaiʻi Review is a literary journal published by the Student Media Board at the University of Hawaiʻi at Mānoa.

Ka Hue Anahā features academic and research writing from various KCC courses, including English, history, philosophy, and psychology.

Newspaper and Magazines

Ka Manaʻo is the student news magazine at Leeward Community College. Students write, photograph, design graphics, edit, and publish the magazine. It also showcases students' creative works such as poetry, art, photography, and creative writing.

Ka ʻOhana is Windward Community College's award-winning student newspaper, a monthly publication that covers both campus and community news.

Ka Leo O Hawaiʻi is the campus newspaper of the University of Hawaiʻi at Manoa.

Kapiʻo News is the student newspaper of Kapiʻolani Community College.

Place-Based Short Stories

Cataluna, Lee. "Kōloa." *Bamboo Ridge*, no. 100, edited by Eric Chock and Darrell H. Y. Lum, Bamboo Ridge Press, 2012, pp. 192-195.

Kanae, Lisa Linn. *Islands Linked by Ocean*. Bamboo Ridge Press, 2009.

Kanae, Lisa Linn. "Born-again Hawaiian." *Islands Linked by Ocean*. Bamboo Ridge Press, 2009, pp. 42-54.

Keller, Nora Okja. "A Bite of Kimchee." *Growing Up Local: An Anthology of Poetry and Prose from Hawai'i*, edited by Eric Chock, James R. Harstad, Darrell H. Y. Lum, and Bill Teter, Bamboo Ridge Press, 1998, pp. 295-299.

Place-Based and Culture-Based Books

Anthologies

Choy, Sammie, et al. *The Best of Aloha Shorts*. Bamboo Ridge Press, 2018.

Literary Criticism

McDougall, Brandy Nālani. *Finding Meaning: Kaona and Contemporary Hawaiian Literature*. University of Arizona Press, 2016.

Poetry

Inoshita, Ann. *Mānoa Stream*. Kahuaomānoa Press, 2007.

McDougall, Brandy Nālani. *The Salt-Wind: Ka Makani Pa'akai*. Kuleana 'Ōiwi Press, 2008.

Passion, Christy, Ann Inoshita, Juliet S. Kono, and Jean Yamasaki Toyama. *What We Must Remember: Linked Poems*. Bamboo Ridge Press, 2017.

"A Brief Guide to Kanaka Maoli (Native Hawaiian) Poetry." Poets.org, Academy of American Poets, 14 May 2004, https://poets.org/text/brief-guide-kanaka-maoli-native-hawaiian-poetry

Toyama, Jean Yamasaki, Juliet S. Kono, Ann Inoshita, and Christy Passion. *No Choice but to Follow*. Bamboo Ridge Press, 2010.

Appendix 3. Additional Suggested Assignments

The assignments listed here include place-based readings and assignments (that is, assignments that use place as a relevant approach and topic). Some of them are culture-based, which means they use the culture, ethnicity, language, and traditions of people groups as engaging and relevant approaches and topics.

Keep in mind that assignments are effective when they use elements that are not only interesting to students but that also encourage them to write about their topic with a strong sense of responsibility to the larger audience or the greater good. Readings and assignments are most ideal when they can be individualized per student, relevant to the student's major area of academic focus, and indeed, to the student's life.

Success Skills for College Learning and Intellectual Growth

Growth Mindset

The Martian (released in 2015, directed by Ridley Scott, and starring Matt Damon), is a film about an astronaut who has been left behind on Mars. Even with efforts to rescue him and bring him home to Earth, he is stranded and must find both a way and his will to survive.

For this assignment, instructors should have students write an essay in which they select a series of specific problems that Damon's character, Matt Watney, encounters.

Then students should explain the decisions Watney makes, the actions he takes, and how his growth mindset helps him overcome challenges so as to live. The way Watney manages his devastating challenges can serve as a model for students to consider when assessing their own challenges and responses.

Note: Instructors should put the film in "closed captioning" mode so students, especially those who are non-Native English speakers, can both hear and see the dialogue (or monologue, as it were).

Before watching the film, students should have read the majority of Carol S. Dweck's *Mindset: the New Psychology of Success*. It might be advisable to have all students read chapters 1-3 and choose one chapter that best suits their lives from chapters 4-7, and have all students read chapter 8.

Further Resources

- Dweck, Carol S. "Carol Dweck Revisits the 'Growth Mindset.'" *Education Week*, 23 September 2015.
- Dweck, Carol S. *Mindset: The New Psychology of Success*, Random House, 2016.

- Dweck, Carol S. "The Power of Believing That You Can Improve," TEDxNorrkoping, November 2014.

Annotation, Close Reading, Rhetorical Analysis

Students should read and annotate the following article written by a student:

Baker, Kaipulaumakaniolono. "Stereotyping Kanaka Maoli–A Stewing Deterrent." *Mānoa Horizons*, vol. 2, no. 1, 2017, pp. 171-175.

With a partner, for 10 minutes (five minutes per student) students discuss what each of them annotated and why. They then take 15 minutes to label the different rhetorical modes and writing strategies the author used in each paragraph, and note how the author used them effectively (e.g., note the impact of the mode or strategy on the reader's understanding of the topic). Next, the class notes and categorizes the modes and strategies used (in a Google Document or on a whiteboard) and discusses how the specific rhetorical mode or writing strategy was particularly effective in its purpose and in addressing multiple audiences. The class also discusses how the essay used diction for power and impact. The discussion can also ask: How does code-switching and multiple "languages" factor into and impact the essay? What kinds of communication powers and issues are observed in the essay? Do all readers respond the same way? If not, how do they respond, and how does the writing affect their response? Is the closing effective in leaving readers with a provocative thought to continue to ponder? During the discussion, students continue to annotate directly onto the printed article or in their notes.

Time Management

Tracking Time and Activity

Students should create a document with 7 columns and 18 rows, labeling the columns from Sunday through Saturday and the rows from 6:00 a.m. to 11:00 p.m., with the 18th row labeled "sleep." They may add additional rows if preferred. For two weeks, students then record what they did every hour. If they worked on English homework for two hours each day, they should label the appropriate starting time with "English" and draw an arrow through two hours of blocked time. If they were in transit for an hour in the morning and an hour in the evening, they should mark the appropriate times "Transportation."

During the third week, students write a two-page reflection on how they spent their time, analyzing how many hours were productive hours in terms of work, school, family responsibilities, and other productive actions; how many hours were leisure hours (spent on social media, video games, shopping, watching movies, surfing, hiking, and so on); whether they were applying 9 hours per week to studying for each of their courses; whether they had enough time to accomplish all they wished to accomplish; and what changes they might have to make during the semester and throughout their college career in order to successfully earn their degrees in their preferred number of semesters (or years).

Essay Structure: Introductions, Body Paragraphs, and Conclusions

Pizza Pie Activity

Prewriting and Thesis

The Pizza Pie activity allows students the opportunity to practice writing an essay while discussing a topic on which they are knowledgeable. Ordering pizza prior to the activity makes for a more "scholarly" activity to engage in this important exercise in truth-seeking to investigate what makes a delicious pizza pie. This activity can take place in two class sessions or as a combination of class work and homework.

- The instructor leads the classroom in a brainstorm (on the board) around what makes a delicious pizza pie.
- After webbing or clustering the ideas in this whole-group exercise, students choose the three most important parts of a pizza. The three popular parts are normally toppings, dough, and sauce.
- The instructor asks the class to create one thesis statement that describes the most important components of a delicious pizza.
- Next, the instructor divides students into three groups. To make things interesting, the three categories can be placed on different slips of papers; one member from each group should choose one.

The Body Paragraphs

- Each group takes a look at their strip of paper and creates a paragraph based on their topic, complete with a topic sentence, supporting sentences, examples, research if preferred, and a summarizing sentence.
- Each group elects a member who types this paragraph into a one Google Document (Google Doc) shared by the whole class and the insructor.
- All of the groups' paragraphs should be entered into a single class Google Doc.

Introductions and Conclusions

- The class should divide into two groups.
- Each group writes either the introduction or the conclusion, using one of the methods discussed in class.
- Each group should continue entering their text into the shared class Google Doc.

Revisions

- With the essay displayed on the Google Doc, each group reads their respective paragraphs aloud.
- The class offers feedback. Instructors and students may use comment features as well as the smart board to make editing suggestions in various colors.
- The team with the best paragraph wins.

Types of Essays

Essays that analyze literature, evaluate writing, and/or apply rhetorical analysis use methods that apply knowledge about writing techniques, textual structures, and rhetorical modes (also known as patterns of development, types of writing, and essay genres) and that analyze the effectiveness of those modes. The key to an analysis-plus-evaluation essay about another essay is to focus on the effectiveness of the writing (and not on tangential opinions about the topics covered in the essay—unless the assignment is about how an essay addresses a topic and what student writers think about that).

Evaluation: Rhetorical Analysis of a Renshi Poem—Four Voices on the Massie Affair

Students should read the four poems from the Bamboo Ridge Renshi Series, an online collection of renshi poetry written by and about Hawaiʻi's people.

In teams of three to four students, students discuss the meaning of these poems and what they reveal about the Massie case in Hawaiʻi. Select one of the following prompts:

- Compare and contrast the diction used in two to four of the poems. How does diction impact the meaning of a line? How does it impact the overall meaning of a poem? Compare how similar words are used in similar ways across the poems. Contrast how similar words are used in different ways. Analyze and discuss the meaning of key words common to all the poems.
- Description: Analyze how the poems describe the Massie case and the people involved.
- Illustration: How are these poems illustrating the challenges faced by Native Hawaiians? What about Asians? What about other people of color? How about Whites? How about military personnel (who may be from various ethnic backgrounds and from various regions and cultures across the U.S. and Hawaiʻi)? Do they connect with contemporary issues faced by the same groups of people today?

Persuasion: Primary Sources, Diction, Vocabulary within Context, and Close Readings—The Reverend Doctor Martin Luther King, Jr.'s Letter from Birmingham Jail

When Dr. King was jailed for protesting against the abuses and systemic discriminatory and racist practices in the United States, he composed an eloquent letter from the jail in Birmingham, Alabama.

King, Jr., Martin Luther. "Letter from a Birmingham Jail," AU, University of Alabama, April 16, 1963.

Students should read and annotate the text. Then select one of the following prompts: Depth, Effort, Format and Persuasion.

Consider the following questions and write a rhetorical analysis of this primary source and the effectiveness of the writing itself.

- What visual rhetoric (particularly formatting) of the original letter reveals the seriousness of this letter? What verbal rhetoric, especially diction, reveals the multiple meanings of the text, and how does that rhetoric do so?
- How do readers know whom the audience is?
- What is the ethos of the speaker?

- What is the kairos behind the diction, syntax, and organization (order of paragraph topics)?
- How would the recipients of the letter know what the main arguments were and what actions Dr. King was asking them to take?
- How does Dr. King add depth to each paragraph?
- What effort, energy, and time were involved in Dr. King's creation of a letter that continues to hold historical and socio-political significance?
- How do all of these factors result in the persuasiveness of this letter, particularly in the eyes of its recipients? How do all these factors affect readers today?
- How do they inform today's community, state, and national leaders and citizens—and non-citizens?

Persuasion: Primary Sources, Diction, Vocabulary within Context, and Close Readings—Queen (Ke Aliʻi Nui) Liliʻuokalani Letter of Protest against the U.S. Assertion of Ownership of the Kingdom of Hawaiʻi

Queen (Ke Aliʻi Nui) Liliʻuokalani wrote this letter to the U.S. House of Representatives to protest the U.S. assertion of ownership of Hawaiʻi, which was recognized by multiple nations as the Kingdom of Hawaiʻi.

Liliʻuokalani. Letter to the U.S. House of Representatives (protesting U.S. assertion of ownership of Hawaiʻi), U.S. National Archives, Records of the U.S. House of Representatives, Record Group 233, Record HR 55A-H28.3, 19 December 1898.

Instructors may use this reading to demonstrate the skills students will demonstrate in argumentative and persuasive research assignments such as the Letter to the Senator. As a means of practicing the persuasive appeals of ethos, logos, and pathos, students color code this letter in groups. Red=ethos, green=logos, and yellow=pathos

Comparison and Contrast

Students should write an essay that compares and contrasts the letters from Dr. King and Queen (Ke Aliʻi Nui) Liliʻuokalani. The essay should also consider following questions:

- What is the power and impact of primary sources? How persuasive are primary sources?
- How powerful can one voice be in effecting change in the world?

Research Skills

Primary Sources

Students should read the following document authored by Miriam Fuchs, a scholar and librarian at the University of Hawaiʻi who described her experiences with and research into the diaries of Ke Aliʻi (Queen) Liliʻuokalani:

Fuchs, Miriam. "The Diaries of Liliʻuokalani." *The Significance of Primary Records*, The Modern Language Association, originally published in *Profession 95*, 1995.

Students should first freewrite answers to the following questions before discussing their answers in groups of three or four:

- What did Miriam Fuchs assume about the diaries, at first?
- How did she find the original primary sources?
- What did the original primary sources reveal?
- What are important considerations when reading other people's accounts of primary sources?
- What is the benefit of reading the primary source?
- What are the impacts of relying only on secondary and tertiary sources?
- What are the benefits of reading secondary and tertiary sources as additions to research in primary sources?
- What primary sources will students find (or have students found) to dive deeper into their research topics? How will they evaluate those sources?

Collaborative Research and Writing Incorporating Debate, Description, Comparison-Contrast, Essay, Slide Presentation, and Debate

Students should first look at, listen to, feel, and smell the wrapper and dimensions of a mini Kit Kat bar and a mini Snickers bar. They should note all the descriptions and observations they can think of, using specific adjectives. As they open each wrapper, they should note and record, in writing, the differences in "experiencing," feeling, and hearing the wrappers as they open, as well as what they smell. As they slowly chew, taste, and experience the different textures of the candies, they should record in writing their observations, always using specific adjectives.

The class will then split down the middle of the classroom, into two groups. One group will argue that Kit Kat is the better candy, while the other argues for Snickers. Each group will compile and organize their lists of observations according to the 5 senses and other observations. They should each brainstorm the many reasons why their candy is better than the other candy. They should then research and evaluate sources, finding professional sources that discuss the merits of each candy, the history of its creation, formulation, and marketing, the nutritional aspects of each candy, and the business practices and philanthropic efforts of each candy company. As each team researches and takes excellent notes (for MLA compliance), the students list additional ways their candy is better than the other candy.

Each team should then brainstorm to build their thesis statements about their claim, as well as argumentation or persuasion techniques, such as how their candy appeals to readers' needs (nutritional value; aesthetic needs, such as through the design of the wrappers; psychological needs, such as the need to include others, share, and belong), emotions (marketing appeals through commercials and print ads), and other rhetorical appeals.

Teams will then brainstorm and draft a CLAIM (a thesis statement expressing the superiority of their candy over the other group's candy and previewing the top reasons and points of comparison). The claim should be written on the board or in a Google Doc, discussed and revised, and the group should ensure consensus and/or compromise.

Debate and Corporate Espionage

To find out what their opponents' claims are, each team will take 7 minutes to present their argument to the other group. Everyone takes notes on the other group's argument, as some people may have different notes from others. Team members can also "listen in" to the other group's conversations if the other group is speaking loudly enough for them to hear. Teams should use their notes on the opponents' counterclaims to brainstorm their essay section that acknowledges the opposing point of view (POV) and then either accommodates or refutes the opposing arguments.

The instructor serves as Supreme Judge and declares the winner of the debate. The winning team takes all the rest of the candy. For homework, the teams progress to their persuasive argument (aka their persuasive essay or argumentative essay).

Food Fight in Cyberspace—Via Collaborative Group Research and Essay

Using team emails and Google Docs, teams should compile their observations, research data, MLA Works Cited citations, draft thesis statements, list of key points, and list of points accommodating and/or refuting their opponents' arguments or claims. Teams should decide on an organizational structure (chronological, priority, spatial) and rank their top key points supporting their claim that their candy is the better candy. Teams should then rank (in a bulleted or numbered list) the other team's strongest arguments, then draft sentences and statements for paragraphs that acknowledge that there's an opposing POV and accommodate and/or refute that opposing POV. They should also review how to successfully write college essays, especially essays using comparison, contrast, description, research, MLA guidelines, and argumentation and persuasion.

Teams should brainstorm topic sentences for all their key points and organize those topic sentences into the outline. Under each outlined topic sentence, they should list their supporting details (data gathered during their observations and from their online research, including the candy corporation websites and professional articles on the companies and the candies).

In their team's Google Doc, each team should create a GRAPHIC ORGANIZER showing the title, thesis, introduction, body paragraphs (with evidence and reasons), and conclusion. Teams may consult their notes and their textbook for examples. Teams should also use brief phrases in the graphic organizer, saving full sentences and transitions for the essay.) Teams should ensure that they have at least one topic sentence and a paragraph summarizing the opposing team's argument. That should be followed by their paragraph that refutes or disproves the opposing team's argument.

An introduction and a conclusion should be brainstormed, so there are now at least 9 paragraphs indicated in the graphic organizer. Each person should select at least 2 paragraphs to collaboratively write with other teammates; teammate choices should overlap so that each person is working on 2 to 3 paragraphs with other teammates, labeling each listed paragraph in the graphic organizer with the names of the writers. (One strategy is to have at least 3 teammates writing paragraphs on more difficult topics; another is to have all teammates collaborate on the introduction and conclusion.) Into the graphic organizer add details that demonstrate the team's TIME MANAGEMENT skills. Set various deadlines for all group members to review the graphic organizer, to agree to the outline, to sign up for sections, to write paragraphs, to review and comment, to edit each other's paragraphs, and to proofread.

Collaborative Writing

Teammates should use the Google Doc COMMENT tool to make suggestions, to ask questions of members and the instructor, and to hold group discussions online. For each topic sentence, the team members responsible draft a paragraph with all the supporting details. They should come up with sweet, solid illustrations (i.e., examples—not drawings) using all 9 patterns of development (rhetorical modes—each paragraph throughout the essay using at least one of the nine). Group members should each collaborate and contribute to their paragraphs by the deadlines they set. The whole team should review the whole essay by the review deadline, using the COMMENT tool to provide feedback, Peter Elbow style. (Highlight or select, click COMMENT, explain what they liked or didn't like about that highlighted or selected section). Team members should review comments on their specific paragraphs and should then respond to—and revise according to—comments by the relevant deadline. The team should also work with their instructor to ensure no instances of plagiarism are indicated. Teams should ensure all outside sources are documented in in-text citations and in the Works Cited list, ensure that paraphrases and data are cited, and ensure everyone wrote in their own words. Everyone should also edit for grammar, punctuation, overall consistency of "voice" and style by the relevant deadline. Everyone should proofread one more time by the relevant deadline for the final battle and final revision.

After their essays are done, teams should create a Google Presentation to accompany their argument and to present to the class on the final day of debate.

CPSIA information can be obtained
at www.ICGtesting.com
Printed in the USA
LVHW061603100821
694994LV00009B/380